PETERHOF

AMFORA
MEDIA LTD.

Dear Guests!

Every summer the palaces and parks of Peterhof are visited daily by thousands of people because there are few places on Earth that are so beautiful. Visitors come here for different reasons: some want to pay their respects to the founder of the "Capital of Fountains" – Emperor Peter the Great; others are interested in the history of the country which takes concentrated form in the former summer residence of the ruling dynasty. People like to learn more about the peculiarities of life at court. Many are drawn by the smaller museums that provide information on a great variety of things – private collections of works of art, playing cards and imperial bicycles, about the extraordinary lives of the famous Benois family and much more.

But whatever the reasons that bring people here, they invariably feel delighted admiration for Peterhof's famous fountains that are looked upon as a sort of calling card of this astonishing place.

Amid the ensemble with the fascinating play of silvery fountain jets the eye is constantly delighted by the resplendent Baroque architecture, the exquisitely finished palace interiors, the park sculpture and the colourful flora of the gardens. All this conspires together to produce a feeling of regret that a summer's day at Peterhof flies by so fast and no-one can manage to do everything in just a few hours: visit more than a score of museums, stroll around the parks and gardens, or go up close to each of the fountains to appreciate its unique appearance.

To slow "time's winged chariot" and provide a memory of Peterhof for you to take away is the purpose of this book – a vade mecum, as the ancients called pocket guidebooks. Translated from the Latin that expression means "come with me" and the staff of Peterhof sincerely invite you to make a fascinating exploration of its remarkable attractions.

The guide has been compiled by a team of people who have made a long and devoted study of the past of Peterhof's sights. It contains brief historical information about them that is intended to add to your enjoyment of your visit and to whet your appetite to learn more and to return to Peterhof with the knowledge that there is plenty of interest still to see. Besides, this book is a worthy addition to any home library, a tangible reminder of time spent in a unique museum ensemble that covers a territory of over 500 hectares and today includes the sights of Strelna, Peterhof and Oranienbaum, each of which is distinct and inimitable.

So come to Peterhof!

Yelena Kalnitskaya

GENERAL DIRECTOR OF THE PETERHOF
STATE MUSEUM-PRESERVE, DOCTOR OF CULTUROLOGY,
HONOURED CULTURAL WORKER OF THE RUSSIAN FEDERATION

HISTORY

PETERHOF is the "world's capital of fountains", the pearl of the Baltic, the triumph of Russian culture embodied in masonry and bronze, the sparkle of jetting water and magnificent landscapes. The artist and art historian Alexander Benois wrote: "Peterhof was born, as it were, from sea foam, as if summoned into existence by a mighty king of the sea… Peterhof is the residence of the king of the seas. The fountains at Peterhof are not an appendage, but the main thing. They are a symbolic expression of the maritime realm, clouds of splashes from the sea that laps [its] shores…"

The first mention of Peterhof (the name means "Peter's court" in German) occurs in 1705 in Peter the Great's campaign journal: "On the 13th day of September our snow [two-masted ship] *Munker* dropped anchor off Peterhof at 4 in the afternoon…" The name Peterhof originally referred to a small manor consisting of a wooden house with outbuildings in which the Tsar stopped for a brief rest during his journeys to view the construction of the forts and fortress on the island of Kotlin that stood guard over the recently founded city of Saint Petersburg. This house was built on the east bank of what is now the Factory Canal, to the west of the Lower Park (close to the Marly).

In 1714, after St Petersburg had been promoted to the status of Russian capital, work began on creating at Peterhof a grand suburban summer residence whose splendour and magnificence would not be inferior to the celebrated summer residences of European monarchs. The creation of the estate took place in the heat of the Northern War (1700–21) which led General Friedrich Wilhelm von Bergholtz, a member of the Duke of Holstein-Gottorp's suite, to remark: "It is incomprehensible how, despite the difficult and drawn-out war, the Tsar was able in such a short time to construct St Petersburg, the harbours at Reval and Kronslot, a considerable navy and so many amusement castles and palaces…"

Peter I was not only the founder, but also the first creator of Peterhof. It was his idea to complete the vista of the entry to the residence from the sea with the "Chambers on the Hill" and a cascade below them. Many technical drawings and sketches made by the great Tsar personally have survived to this day. Some of the best specialists in Europe – architects, sculptors and artists – were invited to take part in this ambitious project: Johann Friedrich Braunstein, Jean-Baptiste Le Blond, Niccola Michetti, Louis Caravaque, Philippe Pillement, Bartolomeo Carlo Rastrelli and others.

The work at Peterhof acquired a truly grand scale after the Tsar's diplomatic visit to France in 1717. The Duc de Saint-Simon wrote at the time: "Peter I, Tsar of Muscovy, has acquired such resounding and deserved fame both in his own country and across the whole of Europe and Asia that I shall not venture to depict this great and glorious ruler, the equal of the greatest men of Antiquity, the wonder of his age, a wonder for the ages to come, the object of the eager curiosity of all Europe."

1

1. Portrait of Peter the Great (Peter I).
Unknown Russian artist after the original by Sir Godfrey Kneller. First third of the 18th century

2. The Great Cascade and Upper Chambers. *Engraving by Alexei Rostovtsev. 1717*

3. View of an Italian Fountain in the Lower Park at Peterhof. *Engraving by Stepan Galaktionov after a drawing by Silvester Shchedrin. 1804–05*

4. View of the Samson Basin with fountains and cascad in the Lower Park at Peterhof. *Engraving by Ivan Chesk after a drawing by Mikhail Shotoshnikov. 1810s*

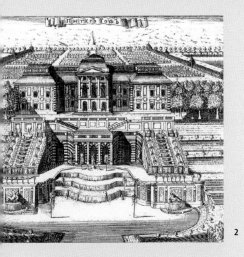

The terrain of the site that Peter chose for the construction of Peterhof was formed by the shelf of an ancient sea (where the Lower Park was laid out, at a height of some two metres above the Gulf of Finland) and a lofty (up to 16 metres high) terrace on the edge of which he placed the palace that was originally known as the Upper Chambers or the Palace on the Hill. It was constructed between 1714 and 1723 under the guidance of Peterhof's first architects: Braunstein, Le Blond and Michetti. This was a fairly small building with three projecting sections of the façade, each topped by a tall tent roof. Its length was equal to the width of the Great Cascade.

At the foot of the palace lay the Lower Park with the Great Cascade descending from the viewing platform to its central section. Within the park the Monplaisir and Marly ensembles were created.

The chief adornment of the parks was the fountains that were supplied with water from the Ropsha conduit, a tremendous feat of engineering whose construction is one of the most important chapters in the history of Peterhof.

Even in the early years of the construction of the residence Peter concerned himself with the problem of providing a sufficient quantity of water for the fountains that he intended to have at Peterhof. Fountains elsewhere were usually supplied by artificial means, using machinery to raise the water, as was the case at Versailles. In 1717 Le Blond presented Peter with a plan that envisaged obtaining a supply from the nearby Hunting Marsh (now Olga's Pond) using a water-mill and a horse-driven machine. That project was, however, rejected, and in August 1720 Peter personally investigated the springs that came to the surface on the northern slopes of the Ropsha Heights, situated 20 kilometres to the south of Peterhof and 70–100 metres above sea-level, and took the decision to construct a canal along which the spring water would flow to Peterhof under the force of gravity.

Construction of the conduit was directed by Vasily Tuvolkov, one of the young men that Peter had sent to Western Europe to study (he acquired his particular skills in Holland and France). By the autumn of 1720 he had managed to plot out the line of the canal, choosing the most advantageous course for the artificial waterway, which involved the least amount of earthwork. During construction they used drainage machines and dredgers made to Tuvolkov's designs. A series of sluices were created to regulate the flow of water and these continue to play an important role today. The construction of the Ropsha Canal was completed by early August 1721 – in just eight months.

On 8 August 1721 Peter I, accompanied by foreign guests and a host of high officials, set off to Ropsha and personally sent the water on its way. At six o'clock in the morning on 9 August "all the fountains and cascades" were put into operation. The grand inauguration of the residence itself followed on 15 August 1723.

After Peter's death in 1725, during the reigns of his widow, Catherine I (1725–27), and his niece, Anna Ioannovna (1730–40), in the main work was carried out in the Lower Park to realize what Peter had already begun or planned.

Peterhof flourished once more in the reign of Peter and Catherine's daughter, Empress Elizabeth (1741–61). The outstanding Baroque architect Francesco Bartolomeo Rastrelli, who was in charge of all the work of reconstructing the imperial residences (the Winter Palace in St Petersburg and the Tsarskoye Selo ensemble as well as Peterhof) to meet the new requirements of representative grandeur, considerably enlarged the Upper Chambers of Peter's day in the years 1747–55. He invested the palace with impressive scope, creating an edifice that extended almost 300 metres along the ridge by enlarging the central Petrine section, which he preserved, and adding galleries on each side that ended into two golden-topped pavilions soaring into the sky – the five-domed palace church consecrated to the apostles Peter and Paul and the Coat-of-Arms Block. The refurbished Peterhof palace amazed visitors with its luxurious magnificence.

The next stage in the history of the ensemble is associated with Catherine II (1762–96). On her orders Yury Veldten – a pupil of Rastrelli, but already a representative of a different tendency in architecture: Classicism that drew on the legacy of traditions from the Ancient World – reconstructed in the new style a few of Rastrelli's halls: the Fore-Hall that became known as the Chesme Hall, the Throne Room and the state dining-room.

When Catherine II's son and heir, Paul I, came to the throne in 1796 the fountain installations at Peterhof were in such poor condition that large-scale reconstruction work had to be carried out. By the time it was complete in 1806, Paul's son Alexander I (1801–25) was already ruler of Russia. It was in this period that another outstanding architect, Andrei Voronikhin, worked at Peterhof. But the palace itself, a brilliant work in the Baroque style, monumental yet at the same time possessing an exquisite silhouette, remained unaltered.

The succession of Emperor Alexander II (1855–81) was marked in Peterhof by the arrival in 1857 of the railway connecting it to St Petersburg.

After the First World War and the revolution the palaces and parks of Peterhof were nationalized and in May 1918 they were turned into museums. Peterhof became one of the country's major centres of culture and public education. But the young Soviet government lacked money and by early 1923 the estate's unique water-supply system had practically ceased to function. A flood in 1924 made the position worse: water from the Gulf of Finland inundated the Lower Park, washing away the shoreline and blocking the fountain basins with sand and silt. In 1925 work on refurbishing the

ensemble began under the direction of the architect A. Shvarts. By 1926 the fountains in the eastern part of the Lower Park had been restored, including the Sun fountain that had not worked for half a century. By 1930 the walls of the Sea Canal and Great Cascade had been rebuilt in parts and the fountain pipes had been replaced, while the overgrown ornamental flowerbeds of the Upper Garden were restored using eighteenth-century drawings.

At the end of September 1941, after stubborn fighting, the Soviet forces were obliged to leave Peterhof. Until January 1944 the town and all its palace-and-park ensembles were occupied by the invaders. Through the heroic efforts of the museum staff, of the 31,000 museum exhibits around 13,000 were saved by evacuation before the Nazis reached Peterhof. On 23 September 1941, the day the town fell, a shell that hit the Church Pavilion set the Great Palace on fire. According to eye-witness accounts the Nazis forbade anyone to fight the blaze on threat of being shot. As a result one of the finest buildings in Europe was reduced to ruins. On 19 January 1944, the day Peterhof was liberated, front-line correspondents reported

4

1. Portrait of the architect Francesco Bartolomeo Rastrelli

2. Portrait of Empress Elizabeth by Carle Vanloo. *1760*

3. Portrait of Emperor Paul I by an unknown artist. *Second half of the 18th century*

4. Portrait of Emperor Alexander I by George Dawe. *1825*

5. King Frederick VIII of Denmark passing through the Roman Fountains parterre. *1909*

a terrible picture of destruction and desolation. Yet as early as the summer of 1946 the grand inauguration of 38 restored fountains took place.

Then in 1948 the decision was taken to reconstruct the palace.

The plan for its recreation was drawn up by two Leningrad architects, Vasily Savkov and Yevgenia Kazanskaya. The first four restored halls were opened in 1964.

Today the fountains, parks and palaces of Peterhof appear before us in all their splendour. The museum is carrying out tremendous work to expand its collections that already number over 150,000 exhibits, while extensive restoration work is still going on, even after returning to life such unique works as the Large and Small Grottoes of the Great Cascade, Olga's and the Tsarina's Pavilions in the Colonists' Park, the Bathhouse Block, the Farmer's Palace and other buildings and installations. New museums have also opened, dedicated to the imperial yachts, the imperial bicycles, the Benois family and collectors, revealing new aspects of the life of magnificent Peterhof.

5

The Great Palace and Great Cascade ↱

THE UPPER GARDEN

THE UPPER GARDEN is an extensive (15 hectare/37 acre) regular French-style park of parterres, a highly typical component of Baroque ensembles and one of the most striking landscapes in Peterhof. Its elegantly regimented composition includes mirror-smooth basins of water, fountains, sculpture and minor forms — little stands of trees (bosquets), trellised arbours and pergolas entwined with plants, splendid flowerbeds, lawns and more.

In Peter I's time this was a fruit and vegetable plot supplying the needs of the palace. It acquired its grand appearance in the reign of Empress Anna Ioannovna (1730–40), when fountain jets were installed in its five basins and sculpture was placed on the paths. Between 1754 and 1760, under Empress Elizabeth, the architect Francesco Bartolomeo Rastrelli completed the decoration of the garden by enclosing it with a fence supported by 150 pillars embellished with cartouches and lion masks.

At that same time the Great Palace of Peterhof was enlarged to his design, its wonderfully harmonious Baroque lines closing off the view on the north side of the garden.

Panorama of the Upper Garden
with the Apollo Cascade
in the foreground

The main entrance gates to the Upper Garden

The Indeterminate Fountain

THE FOUNTAIN closest to the grand gates of the Upper Garden changed its named so often that people took to calling it "indeterminate". It rises in the centre of a circular basin 30 metres in diameter with a rim of dolomite. The main jet in the fountain is decorated with the figure of a sea-dragon surrounded by found playful dolphins. This is all that remains of the original composition, *Perseus and Andromeda*, that was created in 1737 to the design of Bartolomeo Carlo Rastrelli.

The Indeterminate Fountain

The Neptune Fountain

THE MAIN FOUNTAIN in the Upper Garden
is installed in a basin measuring 92 ×
33 metres that was constructed as early
as 1721. Since the late eighteenth century
it has been adorned by the monumental
bronze *Neptune* group — one of the finest
works of the seventeenth-century European
Baroque. It comprises 29 statues and bas-
reliefs and is the oldest assembly of park
sculpture in Peterhof. The composition (by
Christoph Ritter and Georg Schweigger) was
cast in Germany no later than 1660 — before
Versailles became a great residence or Peter
the Great was born — and was supposed to
adorn a fountain in Nuremberg. But for more
than a century it remained dismantled
and in storage. In the 1780s Grand Duke
Paul bought *Neptune* and after he became
emperor (in 1796) he had it installed at
Peterhof.

The Oak Fountain

THE BASIN of this fountain forms a pair with that of the Indeterminate Fountain. The elegant composition adorning its centre takes the form of a little island upon which sits a playful white-marble Cupid trying on a golden mask. Around the island's perimeter are six figures of dolphins (by Bartolomeo Carlo Rastrelli) spurting jets of water. The fountain got its name from a lead oak-tree that stood here in the 1700s (now the Little Oak fountain in the Lower Park). In 1929 marble statues of Zephyrus, Flora, Pomona and Vertumnus (1757; sculptor: Antonio Bonazza) that came from Oranienbaum were set up near the basin.

Zephyrus — the god of the west wind.
Sculptor: Antonio Bonazza. 1757

The Oak Fountain with a sculpture of *A Putto
Putting on a Mask. Sculptor: Giovanni Rossi. 1809*

The Eastern Square Pond

The Square Ponds

THESE TWO ponds, symmetrically placed either side of the main alley of the Upper Garden, were created to Le Blond's design and in Peter I's time served as reservoirs of water. Despite their name they are rectangular (54 × 45 metres) rather than square in shape.

In 1737 the fountain engineer Paul Sualem fitted them with jets that were originally embellished with gilded sculptures by Bartolomeo Carlo Rastrelli. In 1770–73 these were removed and the decoration of the fountains was made crown-like to a design by Ivan Yakovlev. After the Second World War marble statues of Apollo and the Venus Italica were placed in the centres of the fountains. The western Square Pond is part of a splendid corner of the Upper Garden that includes the Coat-of-Arms Pavilion reflected in the smooth water of the fountain basin.

Berceau alley

The vase on the roof of the Great Palace

THE GREAT PALACE

THE GREAT PALACE is a triumphal monument celebrating Russian military victories, the "crown residence" of the Russian empresses and emperors. Still today the lines of its silhouette delight the eye, the exquisite shaped of the tall double-sloped roofs rising to a gilded vase, the fine moulding in the pediments and the wrought-iron work on the balconies incorporating imperial symbols and the monograms of Peter I and Empress Elizabeth.

The northern façade, overlooking the sea, possesses an emphatically grand character. Standing at the top of a 16-metre-high hill, the palace looks a truly monumental, majestic edifice when viewed from the Gulf of Finland.

The line of the façade is broken up by projecting sections that creates a sculptural richness, a play of light and shade from the centre to the side wings with single-storey galleries that end in the east with the five-domed church and in the west with the Coat-of-Arms Pavilion.

The palace halls created by Le Blond, Francesco Bartolomeo Rastrelli and Veldten are amazing for their splendour and refinement, their wealth and abundance of decorative elements.

The Great Palace from the Sea Canal

The Main Staircase

THE STAIRCASE occupies part of a wing specially built by Rastrelli that adjoins the main body of the palace at right-angles. The height of the stairwell is twelve metres, which enabled Rastrelli to create here by 1755 a life-affirming Baroque hymn of praise to the rule of Peter I's daughter, Empress Elizabeth. This interior is stunning for the abundance of light and air, the bold contrasts of colour, the gleam of the gilding, the wealth and expressiveness of the decoration and the variety of lighting effects. The festive impression is enhanced by the ceiling painting, a work by Bartolomeo Tarsia showing the goddess Flora dashing through the clouds in a chariot generously scattering white flower. The walls, window embrasures and coving are decorated with rich ornamental painting (by Antonio Peresinotti). The sumptuous surround to the door into the Ballroom is topped by an imperial crown and allegorical figures of Truth and Mercy. In niches and on the pedestals of the stair-rail are allegorical figures of the seasons. The elegance and refinement of the staircase is underlined by the partly gilded wrought-iron panels of the balustrade (made by the master metalworker N. Stube).

— detail of a ceiling painting:
ress Elizabeth in the Guise of Flora.
y of an original by Bartolomeo Tarsia. 1751

Decorative sculpture: Spring.
After a drawing by Francesco Bartolomeo
Rastrelli. 1749—51

The Ballroom

THE BALLROOM is the apotheosis of luxury, one of the most brilliant interiors created by Francesco Bartolomeo Rastrelli. It has a floor area of 270 square metres (2,900 square feet) but seems considerably larger due to the high flat vault, mirrors and large two-tier windows. The abundance of gilding creates the impression of particular grandeur and brilliance. The woodcarving for this hall was carried out in 1751–52 by Russian craftsmen in the workshop of Josef Stahlmeyer. Broad, elaborately shaped and painted coving frames a gigantic painting that occupies the full area of the ceiling – *Mount Parnassus*, created in 1751 by the Venetian artist Bartolomeo Tarsia and featuring Empress

Tondo: The Rape of Europa by Giuseppe Valeriani. *1740s*

Elizabeth in the guise of Juno. On the walls between the windows are 16 painted tondi by Giuseppe Valeriani on subjects from Ovid's *Metamorphoses* and Virgil's *Aeneid*.

From the middle of the eighteenth century the Ballroom was the setting for palace receptions, balls, masquerades and festivities of which Empress Elizabeth was particularly fond, being unrivalled as a dancer.

The Chesme Hall

THE CHESME HALL is a remarkable memorial to Russia's naval triumphs in the second half of the eighteenth century. It was designed by Veldten in the 1770s on the orders of Catherine II. The saturated dynamism characteristic of Rastrelli's interiors gives way here to balance and a precise articulation of horizontal and vertical divisions. A new material was used in the decoration — stucco moulding (by the craftsmen Nasonov and Bernasconi), which takes the place of gilded woodcarving.

The chief adornment of the hall is twelve large canvases painted in 1771–73 by the German artist Jacob Philipp Hackert. Six of them present episodes in the famous Battle of Chesme (1770), in which the Russian fleet commanded by Count Alexei Orlov inflicted a heavy defeat on the Ottoman navy. There is a bust of Orlov by the Italian sculptor Giovanni Antonio Cibei.

Bust of Alexei Orlov. *Sculptor: Giovanni Antonio Cibei. 1770s*

All the décor of the hall served to extol Russia as a naval power: portraits of ancient heroes and symbols of triumph – the sashes of orders of chivalry wrapped around the picture frames, Turkish weapons, sultans and crescents representing the defeated enemy. The ceiling painting by Augustin Terwesten the Elder also has connections with war and seafaring, being *The Sacrifice of Iphigenia*, one of the episodes leading up to the Trojan War.

The Burning of the Turkish Fleet in Chesme Bay. *Artist: Jacob Philipp Hackert. 1772*

The Loss of the Russian ship *Sviataya Yevstafiya*. *Artist: Jacob Philipp Hackert. 1771*

Vase. *Circa 1830. Imperial Porcelain Factory, St Petersburg*

The Blue Reception Room

RASTRELLI decorated this smaller interior in a comparatively modest manner in keeping with its service function: this was a place of work for secretaries and the officials who kept the journals that recorded events in the life of the court. The walls are lined with a light blue silk fabric that gave the room its name, while the panels and doors are embellished with gilded carving. The walls are harmoniously complemented by a patterned parquet floor, a multi-tiered heating stove entirely covered with blue-and-white tiles and a ceiling painting, *An Allegory of Glory*, by an unknown eighteenth-century artist.

Stylistically closely connected to the interior decoration are the furniture, bronze and porcelain articles that were executed in the "Second Rococo" style, echoing the forms of the mid-1700s. The room contains three canvases depicting the Great Cascade and Great Palace as seen from the Sea Canal. One of them is by the outstanding Russian seascape artist Ivan Aivazovsky.

View of the Great Palace and Great Cascade.
Artist: Ivan Aivazovsky. 1837

Empress Anna Ioannovna. *Artist: Heinrich Buchholtz.*
Last third of the 18th century

Empress Catherine I.
Artist: Heinrich Buchholtz.
Last third of the 18th century

A allegory of Justice.
Sculptor: Ivan Prokofiev.
1770s

Empress Elizabeth.
Artist: Heinrich Buchholtz.
Last third of the 18th century

The Throne Room

THE THRONE ROOM is the largest hall in the palace
(330 square metres, 3,500 square feet). It was
designed by Rastrelli for official receptions, concerts
and balls. In 1777 Catherine II had it redecorated
by Veldten. His project was founded on the idea of
statehood, the theme of civic duty and service to
one's country. The hall is striking for the abundance
of light and air and the eloquence of the decoration.
A background of cold green walls covered with stucco
ornament effectively sets off the formal portraits,
while the crimson patches of the drapes and the
upholstery of the throne adds a solemnly festive
note.

The walls are decorated with reliefs by Ivan
Prokofiev, Mikhail Kozlovsky and A. Ivanov presenting
allegories of Justice, Truth and Virtue together with
episodes from Russian history: *The Baptism of
Princess Olga in Constantinople, Sviatoslav Returning
from the Danube after His Victory* and others.

The patriotic theme is continued in the paintings.
On the western wall are four works depicting the
Battle of Chesme by the English artist Richard Paton.

Between the windows are portraits of members
of the ruling Romanov dynasty beginning with

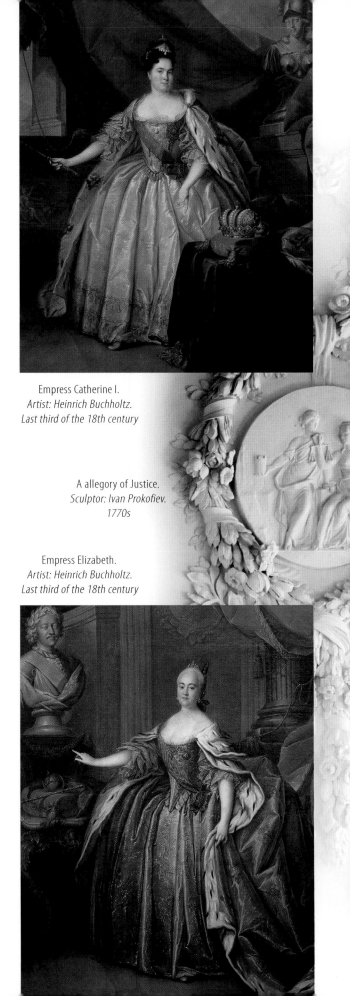

↰ The throne in the Throne Room. *Early 18th century*

Equestrian portrait of Catherine II by Vigilius Erichsen. *1762*

Patriarch Filaret and his son, the first Romanov tsar, Mikhail Fiodorovich. The place above the throne was taken by an equestrian portrait of Catherine II (1762) painted by the Danish artist Vigilius Erichsen specially for this hall. To the sides are copies of portraits of Catherine I, Anna Ioannovna and Elizabeth that Catherine II commissioned from the artist Heinrich Buchholtz.

The throne itself was, according to tradition, made for Peter I to a commission from his closest associate Prince Alexander Menshikov. It is carved oak, gilded and upholstered with red velvet. On the back is a double-headed eagle.

The throne of Nicholas I

The Audience Hall (Room for Ladies-in-Waiting)

THIS HALL, intended as a setting for Empress Elizabeth's audiences, is another of Rastrelli's masterpieces. The play of light in the many mirrors, the gilded windings of the woodcarving and the abundance of candles that intensify the glitter of the gold and the effects of light and shade, the patterned parquet floor and the ceiling painting combined to produce an impression of dazzling luxury. The ceiling painting, made by the Italian Paolo Ballarini in 1754, is a striking perspective work and shows *The Meeting of Rinaldo and Armida*, the final episode in Torquato Tasso's epic poem *Jerusalem Delivered* (1580). On "Kurtäge", days when the palace hosted gatherings of the nobility with concerts, dances, card-games and

dinners, the hall turned into a reception room. Still today card-tables, made by Viennese and German craftsmen in the mid-1700s, stand around its walls.

On display here is a splendid collection of porcelain — acknowledged masterpieces from the Meissen factory. The greater part of the porcelain sculptures were made from models by the celebrated Johann Joachim Kändler. Festively ornate, these figurines accorded with the demands of the Baroque and Rococo styles, elegantly conveying the spirit of the age of gallantry.

Porcelain Vase. *China. 18th century.*
(Bronze mounting — Western Europe, 19th century)

Stucco panel:
Cupids Supporting a Basket
of Fruit

Items from a service made at Josiah
Wedgwood's Etruria factory.
England. 1760s

The White Dining-Room

THIS BRIGHT spacious interior created by Yury Veldten for Catherine II delights the eye with the elegance of its exquisite stuccowork décor executed by Russian craftsmen under the direction of the specialist Bernasconi. The two tall stoves are faced with tiles bearing reliefs that symbolize music and poetry. Oval medallions on the upper part of the walls contain scenes from the ancient myth of Dionysus, the god of viticulture and wine-making and his beloved Ariadne, the daughter of the King of Crete (sculptor: Fiodor Gordeyev).

The large table is set with a service for 30 persons that was made at the Etruria works by the outstanding English potter Josiah Wedgwood. It was commissioned by Catherine II in 1768. The service is complemented by Russian and Bohemian glass from the second half of the eighteenth century embellished with engraving and gilding. The five crystal chandeliers and four girandoles on the table and by the windows were produced by the St Petersburg Glassworks in the 1760s and 1770s.

The Eastern Chinese Cabinet

The Chinese Cabinets

IN THE LATE 1760s two Chinese cabinets
were created by the architect Jean-Baptiste Vallin
de La Mothe on either side of the Picture Hall, the
central room in the Great Palace. Decoration of these
little rooms in a Chinese style was a tribute to a fashion
that had first been introduced in Russia by Peter the Great. The
windows are draped and the walls are lined with damask, yellow
in the western cabinet, crimson in the eastern one. The walls are
adorned with panels from authentic old Chinese screens painted
in gold and silver on a black lacquer background. The subjects are
traditional for Chinese art: landscapes with people going about
their daily business. The decorative painting around the windows,
on the panels, doors and ceilings was executed by the gifted artist
Fiodor Vlasov and his assistants. The elaborate stoves, also the
work of Russian craftsmen, are finished with polychrome tiles.
The impression of exceptional decorativeness is heightened by
the fanciful pattern of the parquet floor assembled from precious
varieties of wood. The cabinets house a collection of Chinese and
Japanese porcelain of the eighteenth and nineteenth centuries,
enamels, and richly inlaid furniture.

Detail of the ceiling
painting in the Western
Chinese Cabinet

Ceramic figure of a Foo dog.
China. 17th century

— The Western Chinese Cabinet

The Picture Hall

THE ROOM, of which Bergholtz wrote "a magnificent hall, whence a splendid view of the sea opens up and one can make out St Petersburg, in the distance to the right, and slightly to the left Kronslot," was the heart of Peter I's Upper Chambers. After Rastrelli's reconstruction it was the last in the Great Palace's suite of state rooms. Today it is an extremely rare example of an eighteenth-century interior with décor that reflects all the stages of the Russian Baroque and Rococo. Originally the hall was known as the Italian Salon. Its walls were hung with tapestries and paintings by Dutch and Flemish artists. Still left from Peter's time are the moulded frieze, the painting on the coving and the ceiling painting – *The History of Hieroglyphics* (1726) by the Venetian artist Bartolomeo Tarsia.

Sculptural dessus-de-porte (over-door composition). *Designed by Francesco Bartolomeo Rastrelli. 1740s*

In the mid-1700s Francesco Bartolomeo Rastrelli added to the décor mirrors, a parquet with an effective diamond pattern and gilded woodcarving. All this combines happily with the paintings executed in the Rococo style by the Italian artist Pietro Rotari. They were placed on the walls "tapestry-fashion" (with no gaps between) in 1764 in an arrangement by the architect Vallin de La Mothe. The exquisite porcelain figurines in the display here are also in the Rococo style. In the late 1840s, when the hall was refurbished, the architect Andrei Stakenschneider replaced the mirrors above the fireplaces and enhanced them with gilded rocaille carving.

The Private Apartments

THE PRIVATE APARTMENTS in the Great Palace of Peterhof are made up of two suites, northern and southern. The northern suite begins with a small drawing-room known as the Partridge Room — one of the interiors that reflect St Petersburg fashion and palace life in the eighteenth century.

The Partridge Room (Boudoir)

THIS ELEGANT boudoir was created by Yury Veldten in the 1770s in the oldest, Petrine part of the palace. Its architectural focus is the partition containing the niche for a divan. It is decorated with gilded woodcarving in the form of hanging garlands, vases, ribbons, medallions containing dancing cupids and other elements. The carving has an elegant lightness about it that gives the room a pleasantly intimate atmosphere.

The Partridge Room served as a sort of music salon and it was where the guests and maids-of-honour waited for the empress to appear after rising. Its colour scheme is based on a combination of light blue, white, greenish and golden tones. Green and white predominate in the decoration of the ceiling, which features the painting *Morning Driving Away the Night*. The silk depicting partridges amongst flowers that was used to line the walls was designed by the outstanding French artist and designer Philippe de Lasalle, known for his splendid fabrics.

Niche containing a divan in the Partridge Room
(the Second Rococo divan dates from the mid-1800s)

The Divin Room

THIS ROOM is located in the projecting section of Peter I's palace that Rastrelli reconstructed to create a bedchamber for Empress Elizabeth with an alcove for her state bed.

In the 1770s Yury Veldten redesigned the room for Catherine II, installing wooden partitions to split it into two — the Divan Room and the Crown Room (p. 49). The elegance of the gilded décor is enhanced by the ornamental painting on the ceiling that was executed by the gifted Russian craftsmen Ivan and Alexei Belsky. The chief adornment of the Divan Room is the eighteenth-century Chinese-made silk on the walls. The silk embroidered with satin stitch on the Turkish divan is a copy of a Chinese fabric, made at Fiodor Korovin's mill in Moscow in the nineteenth century. The interior decoration is complemented by a French-made furniture set from the second half of the eighteenth century and porcelain articles. The latter include a life-size figurine of Zemfira, Catherine II's beloved pet dog, made from a model by Jacques Dominique Rachette in the 1760s.

Niche in the Divan Room

Sculpture: Zemfira.
1779. Imperial Porcelain Factory, St Petersburg

The Dressing Room

THIS FAIRLY SMALL but luxurious room has retained the décor that Rastrelli created for Empress Elizabeth. Only the furnishings and the silk used for the curtains, the wall lining and the upholstery have changed. The fabric stands out for its wealth of intense colours and sumptuous ornamental pattern in which large plant elements are dominant: sprigs of lilac gathered in decorative groups, attractive stylized flowers with fine treatment of light and shade and whimsically curving tendrils of dark blue rocaille. This silk was produced in the nineteenth century at a factory belonging to the merchant Sapozhnikov brothers following an eighteenth-century prototype.

This room was the setting for the rituals of dressing the Empress and preparing her for bed. Only a few were allowed entry here and it was regarded as a mark of particular favour. The exquisite gilded décor goes well with the portraits of Elizabeth, Peter III and Catherine II that hang here. The three-quarter-length portrait of Elizabeth was painted in 1760 from a miniature by Carle Van Loo, one of the foremost Rococo painters and court artist to Louis XV. The work is notable for its especial animation, its idealization and the considerable role played by the accessories. There is another likeness of Elizabeth here — a small equestrian portrait by the German artist Georg Christoph Grooth. It shows the Empress in the uniform of the Preobrazhensky Guards with a sceptre in her hand. A ballet-like grace is introduced into the composition by the elegant Moorish boy-herold standing in a dainty pose in front of his mistress.

The room also contains articles from a porcelain toilet set made in the Second Rococo style at the St Petersburg Porcelain Factory for Empress Alexandra Fiodorovna, the wife of Nicholas I.

Clock. 1840s. Imperial Porcelain Factory, St Petersburg

The Study

THE DÉCOR of the Study dates from the reign of Catherine II and is typical for smaller ornate interiors. The Russian-made writing desk indicates that this was primarily a room for the practical activities of an empress who is known to have had a great passion for literary work (her writings have been published in twelve volumes: fairy tales, pamphlets, plays, memoirs, guidelines on education, translations from Plutarch and whole volumes of her correspondence with Voltaire and Baron Grimm). Here too one can see a host of objects that make the room a cosy living space: the gilded sofa and armchairs (created by the celebrated French maker Georges Jacob), upholstered in the same white silk used to line the walls and indicating that the room was also a place of relaxation, little bronze sculptures and porcelain vases. The Study also contains furniture by Guillaume Beneman, who worked at the court of Louis XVI of France, and the great eighteenth-century German maker David Roentgen. The unique skeleton clock in the form of a lyre made from ormolu and white marble was created by the French craftsman Birdier shows the day and month as well as the time. Clocks of this shape were typical of the second half of the eighteenth century.

On the walls are a landscape by Jacob Philipp Hackert and pictures of Elizabeth, Catherine II and Paul I painted by court portraitists.

Armchair from the workshop of Georges Jacob. *France*

The Passage or Standard Room

IN THE EIGHTEENTH century this was a passage room, in the nineteenth it became the Standard Room as it was the place where the standards of the regiments guarding the residence were kept. Here, as in the Dressing Room and Study the same silk fabric has been used on the walls and the furniture – a typical feature of Russian interiors in the middle and second half of the eighteenth century. The colours of the silk – bright green with rocaille ornament and bouquets of flowers – superbly sets off the gilded carving of the door surrounds that were executed to Rastrelli's designs and gives the room an elevated smartness and cheerfulness. The upbeat character of the interior is enhanced by the portraits hung here. There is an allegorical depiction of Peter the Great with the goddess of wisdom Minerva, painted in London in the 1730s by the Venetian artist Jacopo Amiconi to a commission from Prince Antioch Cantemir, and a portrait of Peter's wife, Catherine I, by an unknown serf artist belonging to Count Sheremetev.

Alongside are portraits of the couple's daughter, Empress Elizabeth (by an unknown eighteenth-century artist) and Catherine II (a replica of the famous portrait made by the remarkable Russian artist Fiodor Rokotov in 1769).

A special role in the decoration of this interior is played by the furniture, notably the light elegant armchairs adorned with carved and gilded ornament and a splendid Russian-made folding table for card-games featuring architectural landscapes skilfully executed in the marquetry technique.

Card table. *Made by Nikifor Vasilyev, Russia. 1770s*

The Cavaliers' Room

THIS ROOM gets its name from the fact that it was used by the elite Cavalier Guards who kept watch over the private apartments. Its décor, designed by Francesco Bartolomeo Rastrelli, includes such elements as a parquet floor with a zigzag pattern, sumptuous door surrounds and a large tiled stove. The walls are lined with a dark crimson silk framed with gilded beading. A large portion of the objects that were in this room up until the war were not evacuated and perished. Specialists have now chosen furnishings for it that were characteristic of such palace interiors in the eighteenth century. The paintings on the wall are mainly battle scenes. Most notable among them is a *Cavalry Battle* by the eminent French painter Adam-François van der Meulen, court artist to Louis XIV.

The Small Passage Room

THE WALLS of this tiny room are lined with a magnificent silk featuring bouquets framed with garlands of flowers that was woven in the 1840s at the Sapozhnikov factory. On the walls are a *Portrait of an Old Man* by the outstanding Italian master Giovanni Battista Tiepolo, a *Portrait of Vittoria Accoromboni* by Scipione Pulzone, a prominent Italian Mannerist of the second half of the sixteenth century, and also a Flemish work of the second half of the seventeenth century — *The Apotheosis of War*, which is easily recognized as being in the style of the studio of the great Peter Paul Rubens.

The Large (Blue) Drawing-Room

THIS DRAWING-ROOM provides a very ornate conclusion to the northern suite of private apartments. It was decorated in the mid-eighteenth century to plans by Rastrelli, who based his approach on the energetic design of the gilded woodcarving and the multicoloured ornamental painting on the broad coving (1753; artist: Login Doritsky). These elements contrast powerfully with the blue silk used for the curtains, walls and upholstery.

In the south-east corner of the room is a multi-tiered stove decorated with little columns and gilded lead figures and faced with tiles painted with Dutch landscapes and genre scenes in cobalt blue on a white background. Tiles like these were made by Russian artisans at St Petersburg's brickworks under the guidance of the master craftsman Willem Elbrecht.

The dessert part of the Banquet service

This room was used for meals for a small number of diners. So the main element of furnishing are tables now used to display items for the Baquet Service for 250 persons that was made at the Imperial Porcelain Factory in 1848—53 specially for the Great Palace at Peterhof. In the service the Russian artists — Fiodor Krasovsky, Yegor Maximov and others — used the "cabbage leaves" motif that adorned the French Sèvres Service of the 1760s, yet at the same time created original objects that were varied in shape. The decoration of the tables also includes vases and glasses in the strict Classical style of the 1820s made from clear lead crystal glass at the Imperial Glassworks.

Catherine II as Legislator in the Temple of Themis.
Copy by an unknown late 18th-century artist of a 1783 painting by Dmitry Levitsky

Candelabrum.
Mid-19th century

The stateliness of the Large (Blue) Drawing-Room is enhanced by formal portraits of Catherine II (a copy of a work by Dmitry Levitsky), Grand Duke Peter Petrovich (the future Peter III; after 1743; a copy of a work by Georg Christoph Grooth) and Grand Duchess Maria Fiodorovna (possibly by Elisabeth Vigée-Lebrun).

The room contains late eighteenth-century French furniture (a sofa and armchairs), cupboards in the Louis XVI style by Barbedienne, one of the foremost craftsmen of the mid-nineteenth century, and other pieces.

The Secretary's Room or Choir Anteroom

THE SECOND name for this small
service room comes from its
position next to the choir galleries
of the Palace Church. A door from
the Secretary's Room leads onto
the eastern gallery and from there into
the church itself.

Chandelier. *1851.*
Imperial Porcelain
Factory, St Petersburg

The decoration of the room was carried
out in the mid-1700s to Rastrelli's designs.
The post-war restorers recreated the zigzag parquet floor
typical of the architect, restored the carved panels,
the gilded window embrasures, the tiled stove and also the
stylish silk on the walls.

The interior is adorned by some splendid pieces created at the
Imperial Porcelain Factory in the middle of the nineteenth century –
a chandelier for 48 candles and decorative vases with ormolu mounts.

Vase. 1854–57. Imperial Porcelain
Factory, St Petersburg

47

The First Room of the Spare Apartment

The Second Room of the Spare Apartment

The Rooms of the Spare Apartment

THE LARGE (Blue) Drawing-Room connects the northern suite of the palace with the Concert Hall and the southern suite that comprises four rooms belonging to "Olga's Apartment" that were redecorated in 1845–46 in the Second Rococo style by the architect Andrei Stakenschneider. The rooms that in the eighteenth century had no particular function were being prepared for Nicholas I's daughter Olga on the occasion of her marriage to the Prince of Württemberg. Stakenschneider decorated them gilded carving and fabrics woven at the Kondrashov and Sapozhnikov factories in Moscow. Here too there is a collection of applied art including porcelain from the Imperial Factory, bronze from the Petersburg-based Chopin company, furniture from the celebrated workshops of Tur and Gambs.

Later the rooms became a sort of court hotel for distinguished foreign guests.

Today there is a considerable display of paintings by Western European artists of the seventeenth to nineteenth centuries, including large formal portraits of Nicholas I and his daughters by the English artists George Dawe and Christina Robertson, European and Russian furniture and porcelain from the second half of the eighteenth century and early nineteenth, artistic bronze.

The Crown Room

The Third Room of the Spare Apartment

THE CROWN ROOM, like the Divan Room on the north side to which it is connected by doors, was created in the mid-eighteenth century to Rastrelli's design, then reworked in the 1770s by Yury Veldten. The two rooms are practically a matching pair: here too there is a partition with an alcove, and the walls are lined with painted Chinese silk (in this case depicting the process of making porcelain at the Chinese imperial factories at Jingdezhen).

Originally this room was known as the Bedchamber, although it was never used as such. Its presence in the suite of state rooms was intended to underline the exalted status of the palace's owners. It became the Crown Room during the reign of Paul I when a stand for the imperial crown was installed here.

Italian gueridon table with a marble mosaic top. *18th century*

The Oak Study
of Peter the Great

THE STUDY has retained almost completely the appearance it had in Peter I's time. It is known to have been designed by Jean-Baptiste Alexandre Le Blond, one of the greatest European architects to work at Peterhof in its founder's time. It was Le Blond who suggested using wooden panels with figurative carving to decorate the room. The Study is therefore a unique historically authentic example of the decoration of Russian palace interiors in the first

Carved panel bearing an allegorical depiction of Peter I

quarter of the eighteenth century. Bergholtz wrote of it in his *Diary*: "Particularly remarkable is the study, where the Tsar has a small library consisting of various Dutch and Russian books. It was finished by a certain French sculptor and is notable for its superb carved decorations." The sculptor was the highly talented Nicolas Pineau.

The items in the study include Peter I's personal travelling alarm-clock, made by the German craftsman Johannes Benner. Glazed panels on its sides allow you to see the mechanism working. On the flap of the desk is a book of *Peter the Great's Decrees from 1714 to 28 January 1725*, published in 1739.

Cabinet (tabletop secretaire).
Ebony, semiprecious stone, ivory. South Germany. 18th century

The Oak Staircase

UNTIL RASTRELLI'S reconstruction of the palace the main staircase in the Upper Chambers was the Oak Staircase, situated, as was always the case in Peter's residences, in the centre of the building. Like the Oak Study this staircase was created to Le Blond's design in 1722–26. Here too the main finishing material is oak. Nicolas Pineau was involved in the decoration work. The ceiling painting above the stairwell depicts Aurora, the goddess of the dawn, and is the work of the Russian artist Ivan Vishniakov. The subject symbolizes the dawn of a new era in Russian history — the era of Peter's reforms.

Portrait of Peter I by Benoit Coffre. *1716*

The Church Pavilion

WHEN PLANNING the reconstruction of the Upper Chambers, Francesco Bartolomeo Rastrelli included in the ensemble the Church Pavilion, a fairly small place of worship for the court connected to the palace by a gallery. The 27-metre-high church was topped, as Empress Elizabeth wished, with five domes and included an altar dedicated to the apostles Peter and Paul and a refectory.

The domes of the pavilion were embellished with decorative carving executed in 1749 under the supervision of C. Girardon. The church is notable for the fact that here, on 11 August 1904, the last heir to the Russian throne – Nicholas II's son, Tsesarevich Alexei – was baptised.

Interior of the Church of SS Peter and Paul in the Church Pavilion. *Artist: Eduard Hau. 1842* →

The Crimson Drawing-Room

The Coat-of-Arms Pavilion

RASTRELLI constructed and decorated this pavilion in 1745—50, at the same time as the Church. The rich expressiveness of its lines, its exquisite proportions, the plasticity of the masses and the clarity of the volumes also place it among the most striking achievements in European architecture in the mid-seventeenth century. The pavilion takes its name from the weathervane that crowns it that was made by Girardon in the form of a heraldic eagle from a model and drawing by Rastrelli. The eagle was given three heads, but from any viewpoint it seems to have two. The gilded decorative carving on the dome and the cupola above it was executed under the guidance of the master craftsman Josef Stahlmeyer in 1751.

The rooms inside the building were also finished in the mid-1700s to designs by Rastrelli (with the participation of Stahlmeyer, Bernhard Egg, A. Voronin, I. Sidorov, Willem Elbrecht and others).

In the 1750s this pavilion was given over to the "lesser court" of the heir to the throne, Grand Duke Peter Petrovich, and his wife, Catherine Alexeyevna. Later it became accommodation for junior members of the imperial family and exalted guests visiting Peterhof.

Today the pavilion's eight rooms house Peterhof's Special Treasury — a collection of memorial items that belonged to Russian rulers from Peter I to Nicholas II, and also a collection of paintings, unique court costumes, furniture, pieces of jewellery and more.

The Vestibule

The Cabinet

The Interiors of the Coat-of-Arms Pavilion

THE MAIN DISPLAYS of the Special Treasury are located in the grand reception rooms of the northern suite. A tour begins with the Entrance Hall, where the most interesting exhibits are former belongings of Peter the Great: a silver sundial, a ship's chronometer that was a present from King George I of Britain, the Tsar's snuffbox, a dress uniform and more.

From the Entrance Hall visitors move on to the Crimson Drawing-Room that begins the northern suite. This room was used as a place to prepare for the grand processions through the galleries and rooms of the palace to the church. The display here contains examples of formal court attire, precious accessories and magnificent thrones used by Empress Maria Fiodorovna (the wife of Alexander III) and her son, Nicholas II.

Next comes the Yellow Drawing-Room that is lined with silk that was chosen personally by Nicholas I in 1846, during the preparations for the wedding of his daughter, Olga. Presented in this room are costumes and items for leisure use. Here too you can see a saddle, harness and bridle presented by Empress Elizabeth to Catherine Alexeyevna (the future Catherine II).

The northern suite continues with the private apartments of Catherine II: her Study, Bedroom and Dressing-Room. On display in the Bedroom are some of the Empress's belongings that she personally used. The elegant Dressing-Room that completes the northern suite contains a silver mirror (made by François-Thomas Germain) that was probably a part of a toilet set presented to Empress Elizabeth by Louis XV of France.

Chandelier. *Poland.*
19th century

Ink stand that belonged to Alexander I.
Made by A. Hedlund. 1800–10

Silver frame with
a portrait of Peter I.
*Made by Charles
Boit. 1717*

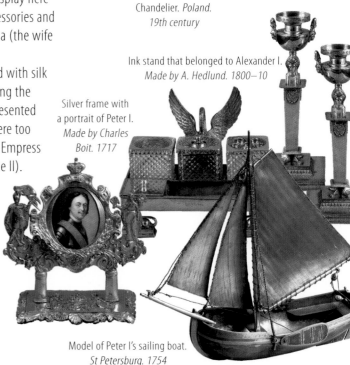

Model of Peter I's sailing boat.
St Petersburg. 1754

Presentation snuffbox commemorating
the Russian victory at Kunersdorf
during the Seven Years' War.
England. 1759

Fan. *Western Europe.*
1840–50
Fan. *France. 1770*

The last rooms of the exhibition are the Corridor,
housing a display of ecclesiastical items, and the Jeweller's
Room that presents the history of that craft in Russia and
contains examples of the jeweller's art including some that
come from the world-famous workshops of Carl Fabergé.

The Dressing Room. The Dressing Mirror.
Jeweller: Francois-Thomas Germain, Paris. 1750s

The Bedroom (*architect: Yury Veldten*). The armchair in the
centre was made by Jean-Baptiste Tilliard (*Paris, 1770s*)

The Trumpeting Tritons fountain

THE GREAT CASCADE

THE GREAT CASCADE is Peterhof's chief adornment — a grand, magnificently decorated monument to Russia's victories in the Northern War, a unique artistic ensemble of world significance.

The architectural basis of the cascade is a grand spreading "staircase" (with an area of about 300 square metres) on which there are over 70 fountains and some 250 sculptures and bas-reliefs made of bronze, lead and marble. With its dimensions, its wealth of sculptural decoration and, last not least, the astonishing unity and expressive power of all the elements of the ensemble, it occupies one of the leading places among the world's fountain installations.

Surviving rough sketches made by Peter I personally are evidence that he was the person who came up with the idea of the cascade. Its construction, which involved the architects Braunstein, Le Blond, Michetti and Zemtsov as well as the fountain specialist Paul Sualem, lasted from 1715 to 1724. Improvements to the ensemble were made over the next century and a half.

The Lower Grotto. Central Hall

Fountain mask.
18th century

The Large (Lower) Grotto

THE FAMOUS grottoes (a word of Italian origin for a small natural or artificial cavern) — Lower and Upper, or Large and Small — give the Great Cascade a special mysterious fascination. The Large Grotto is the heart of the cascade. From the broad platform in front of it the waters fall in a silvery veil down ledges into the basin below.

Fountain mask. 18th century

Construction of the grotto began in the spring of 1715 under the direction of Le Blond and was continued by Braunstein and Michetti. The structure is nine metres high. Its outer wall extends for over 40 metres and is pierced by five archways that have keystones in the form of gilded masks. Outside and inside the grotto is faced with tufa. Its interior is adorned with gilded statues (installed in the 1860s) and four marble busts representing the seasons: *Winter* and *Spring* by Pietro Baratta, *Summer* and *Autumn* by an unknown Italian sculptor of the first half of the eighteenth century. In 1728–29, after Peter I's death, but to his design, a "stone table with splashing" featuring a water-operated bronze basket was installed and "watery curtains" constructed at the exit (architect: Piotr Yeropkin, 1727).

The Lower Grotto. Pan and Olympius. *Galvanoplastic copies of ancient originals. Workshop of J. Hamburger, St Petersburg, Russia. 1857*

The Lower Grotto. Bust of Spring. *1718–20*

In front of the grotto the *Wheel* fountain was constructed to Peter's design. In 1860 the pattern of its jets was made rather more elaborate after which the fountain became known as the *Basket*. Twenty-eight inclined interweaving jets spurt from a ring of tufa. It seems as if pearly tulips have been gathered in a crystal basket. In the language of allegory this fountain symbolizes the wealth and might of the Russian state.

The Small (Upper) Grotto

CONSTRUCTION of the Small or Upper Grotto began in 1716 under the guidance of Michetti, Le Blond's successor. The completion of the work was registered in 1723. On the sides of the outer face of the grotto there are two wall-fountains decorated with masks of Neptune and Bacchus (each about 2 metres high) that watch over the entrance to the grotto. The masks were created by Bartolomeo Carlo Rastrelli from a drawing by Mikhail Zemtsov. Here too, in shallow niches, there are marble busts representing the seasons.

Bas-reliefs: Diana and Actaeon and Sacrificial Offering

Vase on the balustrade of the Upper Grotto. *After a drawing by Andrei Voronikhin. 1800*

Sculpture: Amazon. *After an ancient original from the 4th century BC.*
Sculpture: Jupiter. *After a model by Jacques Dominique Rachette. 1801*

The Sculpture of the Great Cascade

THE THEME of Russia's maritime triumph is expressed
above all in the sculptural decoration of the cascade.
The watery extravaganza opens with muscular Tritons,
the lords of the waves, blowing a fanfare to Russian
victories on conch-shell trumpets. It ends with the
mighty Samson.

The original sculpture was produced
to drawings by the architects Le Blond
and Braunstein in England and Holland,
as well as St Petersburg, where
Bartolomeo Carlo Rastrelli and François
Vassou worked on it.

Top — Callipyg
Venus. *Afte*
an ancient
original.
1800

Pandora.
After a model
by Fedot Shubin.
1801

Perseus.
After a model
by Feodosy Shchedrin.
1801

Capitoline Mercury. *Copy of an ancient original. 1800*

By 1723 the sculptural decoration included 16 gilded lead figures. By the end of the eighteenth century the lead statues had become deformed under the influence of the water and in 1799 a commission from the Academy of Arts acknowledged the need to replace them with bronze ones. This work was completed in 1806. Of the 32 new statues made, 15 were originals, while the others were copies of ancient sculptures. The original works were created by such eminent sculptors as Ivan Prokofiev (*Tritons*, *The Volkhov* and *Acis*), Feodosy Shchedrin (*Perseus*, *The Neva*, *Sirens*), Ivan Martos (*Actaeon*), Fedot Shubin (*Pandora*) and Jacques Dominique Rachette (*Galatea*, *Jupiter*, *Juno* and *Naiads* and *Tritons*).

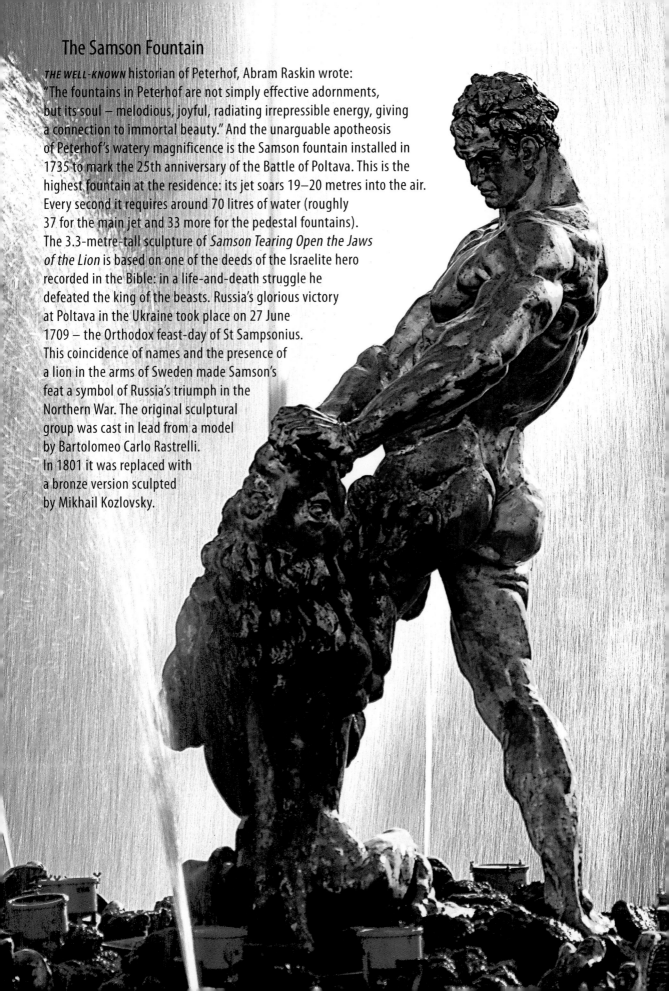

The Samson Fountain

THE WELL-KNOWN historian of Peterhof, Abram Raskin wrote:
"The fountains in Peterhof are not simply effective adornments,
but its soul – melodious, joyful, radiating irrepressible energy, giving
a connection to immortal beauty." And the unarguable apotheosis
of Peterhof's watery magnificence is the Samson fountain installed in
1735 to mark the 25th anniversary of the Battle of Poltava. This is the
highest fountain at the residence: its jet soars 19–20 metres into the air.
Every second it requires around 70 litres of water (roughly
37 for the main jet and 33 more for the pedestal fountains).
The 3.3-metre-tall sculpture of *Samson Tearing Open the Jaws
of the Lion* is based on one of the deeds of the Israelite hero
recorded in the Bible: in a life-and-death struggle he
defeated the king of the beasts. Russia's glorious victory
at Poltava in the Ukraine took place on 27 June
1709 – the Orthodox feast-day of St Sampsonius.
This coincidence of names and the presence of
a lion in the arms of Sweden made Samson's
feat a symbol of Russia's triumph in the
Northern War. The original sculptural
group was cast in lead from a model
by Bartolomeo Carlo Rastrelli.
In 1801 it was replaced with
a bronze version sculpted
by Mikhail Kozlovsky.

The Pyramid Fountain

THE LOWER PARK

THE GREAT CASCADE is a link between the Great Palace and the ensemble of the Lower Park – an outstanding work of landscape design with a regular geometrical layout.

The park has an area of 112.5 hectares (280 acres). It incorporates three local palace ensembles (Monplaisir, Marly and the Hermitage) and is adorned by four cascades (including the Great Cascade) and over 150 fountains.

The park is laid out on a narrow strip, some two kilometres by 500 metres, along the coast of the Gulf of Finland and is bounded on the south by a natural terrace 14–16 metres high. On the terrace either side of the Great Cascade are ten small cascades with water descending in steps to stone bowls above which thin jets of water rise. These compositions, known as the Terrace Fountains, were created in 1799–1801 by the architect Franz Brouer and fountain engineer Fiodor Strelnikov to a design by Andrei Voronikhin. Originally the steps were made of Pudost limestone, but in the 1850s Andrei Stakenschneider replaced them with marble.

The Great Parterres

The Great Parterres. The *Danaid* fountain

The Great Parterres

LAID OUT symmetrically on the broad open area at the foot of the Great Cascade are the twin Great Parterres (ornamental arrangements of flowerbeds), the most formal part of the Lower Park. The parterres were created under the direction of the master gardener Bernhard Fock and each is divided up by wide paths into four separate flowerbeds.

In the centre of the parterres are the *Bowl* fountains with 10-metre jets – the western *Italian* (the Italian Baratini brothers took charge of its construction) and the eastern *French* (created by the French specialist Paul Sualem). The *Bowls* were made in 1721–22 following a plan by Michetti. In 1854 the architect Andrei Stakenschneider had the fountain bowls and basins remade in Carrara marble.

One of the Voronikhin colonnades

On the north side the beds of the parterres are bounded by the finely proportioned Voronikhin Colonnades erected to replace dilapidated wooden ones in 1800—03 to the design of Andrei Voronikhin. The flat roofs of the colonnades also serve as fountain basins. They contain gilded bronze bowls from which silvery jets of water rise.

More fountain compositions are situated in the north-west and north-east corners of the parterres. These are the *Marble Bench* fountains (1850s; design by Stakenschneider): *Nymph* on the west side and *A Dainaid* on the east.

To the west of the Great Parterres lies the Sandy Pond that was dug out under the supervision of Vasily Tuvolkov in 1724—27. In 1740 a fountain was installed in the centre of the pond that was decorated with a sculpture of a "whale-fish". This adornment was later removed, but the name *Whale Fountain* survived.

The Whale fountain

The Orangery Garden

TO THE EAST of the Great Parterres a short path leads to the small Orangery Garden, a complex of hothouses from the Peterhof of its founder's time.

The history of this area goes back to March 1722, when Peter I gave orders "to build an orangery on the place the gardener indicated." The design was probably the work of the architect Michetti, while construction, in 1722–25, was overseen by Johann Friedrich Braunstein. Despite its functional purpose the building of the Orangery has the look of a smart palatial pavilion.

The Orangery became the centre of a garden, whose chief adornment in the fountain of *A Triton Tearing Apart the Jaws of a Sea-Monster*. This work symbolizes the young Russian navy inflicting a defeat on a Swedish squadron at Cape Gangut (Hankö) on 27 July 1714. The sculpture was created in 1726 from models by Bartolomeo Carlo Rastrelli at the same time as the fountain basin was constructed (architect: Timofei Usov; fountain engineer: Paul Sualem).

The *Triton* fountain in the Orangery Garden

A panorama of the parterre garden below the Chessboard Hill cascade

The Roman Fountains

THESE FOUNTAINS adorn a parterre in the eastern part of the Lower Park that was laid out in the mid-1700s by the gardener Bernhard Fock, who created sunken "bowling-green" lawns here. The idea for the fountains goes back to Peter's time, but they appeared in the park only in 1739 to the design of Karl Blank and Ivan Davydov who copied in wood the composition of stone fountains on St Peter's Square in Rome. In 1763 the fountains were moved to their present sites — on the axis of the Birch Alley — and abundantly decorated

Mask on a Roman Fountain

with carved and gilded details. In 1800 they were rebuilt in granite and marble. The work was overseen by the architect Franz Brouer assisted by the fountain engineer Fiodor Strelnikov. They fitted each construction with five jets, the central ones rising to a height of 2–5 metres. Seventeen years later the fountains were embellished with new bronze masks cast from models by the sculptor Ivan Martos. The fountain basins have remained unaltered since 1739.

The Chessboard Hill Cascade

THIS CASCADE is situated on the slope of the terrace descending to the parterre with the *Roman Fountains*. The water pours onto its steps from the jaws of dragons guarding the entrance to the upper grotto. The steps are flanked by white marble statues made by early eighteenth-century Italian sculptors of characters from ancient mythology – Neptune, Jupiter, Andromeda, Flora, Pomona, Ceres, Vulcan and Pluto.

The concept for this installation was devised by Peter the Great, who made a fairly detailed description of the composition inspired by the Small Cascade at the French royal residence of Marly. Between 1722 and 1728 the architects Braunstein, Michetti, Zemtsov and Usov were all involved in creating the cascade. In 1738 a new project for its

decoration devised by Johann Blank and Ivan Davydov was approved. It was then that the cascade was embellished with painted wooden figures of dragons (made from models by Konrad Ossner), while the main finishing materials became tufa stone and oyster shells. In 1769 the wooden steps of the cascade were replaced and painted chessboard-fashion, after which it was known as both the *Dragon Hill* and the *Chessboard Hill*. In 1874 the wooden dragons were replaced with lead ones made to a drawing by Nikolai Benois.

The Pyramid Fountain

THE FIRST mention of a "water pyramid with little cascades" came in 1721, when on Peter I's orders the architect Michetti produced a technical drawing for a reproduction of the *Obelisk* fountain at Versailles. But the Tsar decided to change the shape of the figure, making it four-sided instead of three. The work was completed in 1724 under the direction of the architect Mikhail Zemtsov and the fountain engineer Paul Sualem. The Holsteiner Bergholtz wrote in 1723: "There is not another such large and beautiful water jet perhaps anywhere." Today it is the most lavish fountain consuming over 150 litres every second. An arrangement of 505 nozzles forms an eight-metre four-sided seven-stepped foaming pyramid of water – an unusual monument to the conclusion of the Northern War in 1721. In 1768 the architect Yakov Alexeyev produced a design for a graite surround to the fountain that was implemented in 1799, then in 1800 craftsmen of the Peterhof Lapidary Works made the marble elements of the *Pyramid's* basin and balustrade.

The Eastern Maze

TO THE SOUTH-EAST of the *Pyramid* fountain in 1721–23 Peter the Great had a maze created that was based on a standard design in a French eighteenth-century book on the theory and practice of gardening. Restored in 2008–09 together with a 7.6-hectare area of the Lower Park, the *Maze* consists of 16 boskets (stands of trees) surrounded by lime espaliers. In the centre is a small oval area with a basin lined with natural stone and a fountain. Inside the large boskets are figured areas with benches.

The Monument to Peter the Great

A PATH running north-west from the *Maze* past the *Pyramid* leads to the Marly Alley that is fringed with trimmed lime (linden) trees. This is the longest alley in the Lower Park (2 km). At its junction with the Monplaisir Alley on 8 May 1884, to mark the 200th anniversary of Peter I's birth, a monument was unveiled to the great founder of Peterhof. It was created by the sculptor Mark Antokolsky (with a granite pedestal designed by the architect Eduard Hahn). The bronze figure is about 2.8 metres tall, the pedestal 3 metres. The Emperor is shown in the uniform of the Preobrazhensky Guards in which he led his forces into the attack against the Swedes at Poltava, with the sash of an order of chivalry across his shoulder. His imperious gaze is directed out to sea, towards the Kronstadt fortress that he founded and his new capital — St Petersburg.

The Sun Fountain

FROM THE MONUMENT to Peter I the Monplaisir Alley runs north to that Tsar's favourite palace — Monplaisir. On the way is another ensemble from the founder's era — the Menagerie Garden that was created in 1719 by the architects Le Blond and Braunstein for the menagerie that Peter planned. The main sight of this garden in the *Sun* fountain that has a history going back to 1721 when the Tsar gave orders to "make a fountain in the pond where the menagerie is."

In June 1723 the fountain designed by Michetti was completed and tested with water. Peter had it modified several times. In 1772 to the design of the architect Yury Veldten (assisted by Ivan Yakovlev) the fountain was made in the form

of a rotating column attached to the top of which was a
construction with 187 openings. The jets of water emerging
from them resembled the rays of the sun and so the
fountain acquired its present name. Today it is a very
rare surviving example of an eighteenth-
century mechanical fountain.

The Aviaries

THE AVIARIES adorned the Menagerie Garden in keeping with a tradition that went back to the sixteenth and seventeenth centuries, when it was fashionable to have poultry farms and dovecotes on country estates. The aviaries in the Menagerie Garden take the form of elegant 12-sided pavilions covered with domes topped by lanterns. The walls between the windows of the pavilions are decorated with oyster shells, tufa and dross (the waste from iron-smelting). The design of the aviaries has been attributed to the architect Michetti.

Inside the aviaries are decorated with polychrome painting (in oils and tempera on a wooden base with highlights worked in gold) believed to be by Louis Caravaque. Besides the ornamental work, in the western aviary there is also narrative painting on the theme of the myth of Diana and Actaeon, which was popular in Peter I's time. In the eighteenth century cages containing songbirds were placed in the aviaries each summer: nightingales, thrushes, longspurs, siskins, chaffinches, redpolls, bullfinches, exotic parrots, canaries and others. For peafowl and pheasants large wire enclosures were set up. The birds were moved for the winter to the Poultry Farm located to the west of the Marly area.

Today the aviaries are again home to birds: parrots in the eastern one and songbirds (nightingales, thrushes, goldfinches, siskins, amadinas and others) in the western.

Next to the eastern aviary for the anniversary year of 2005 the old Swan Pond was restored. Now swans, Canada geese, Mandarin ducks and ruddy shelducks can be seen swimming on it.

Decorative painting on the dome of the eastern Aviary

The *Little Oak* trick fountain. *Sculptor: Bartolomeo Carlo Rastrelli. 1735*

The *Pet Dog* trick fountain. *Architect: Mikhail Zemtsov. Sculptor: Konrad Ossner. 1725*

The Trick Fountains

ONE of the most interesting features of the eastern part of the Lower Park is the trick fountains, the fashion for which Peter the Great brought back from abroad where such amusements were particularly popular at the court of Louis XIV.

One of the oldest practical jokes of this sort at Peterhof — the "Water Road" — was created by Michetti on the Monplaisir Alley. In the Peterhof archives some notes from Peters the Great survive in which he urges that this installation be completed "quicker, quicker, quicker..." The fountain was first started up in 1721.

Another of the trick fountains — the *Umbrella* — was constructed in 1796 in the Menagerie Garden to the design of the architect Franz Brouer. Around the perimeter of its wooden "cap" there are 164 little tubes hidden behind the carved festoons.

Across the alley from the *Umbrella* stand the *Little Oak* fountain that was moved here from the Upper Garden in 1802. Originally the "oak" (produced

to Bartolomeo Carlo Rastrelli's design in 1735) was gilded. The fountain engineer Fiodor Strelnikov turned it in a "natural tree" and encircled it with "tulips", while placing two wooden benches close by. Behind each of the benches 41 tubes are hidden, from which water spurts out to splash the distracted visitors.

Close to the *Little Oak* are other trick trees — the *Little Firs*. These were installed in 1784 by Strelnikov and his colleague J. Kaiser and take the form of little metal conifers painted natural colours. Fine jets of water squirt from their branches.

The *Umbrella* trick fountain. *Architect: Franz Brouer. 1796*

One of the two trick benches in the Monplaisir Garden

Monplaisir

MONPLAISIR from the French for "my pleasure") was the first palace-and-park ensemble to be created at Peterhof. Peter the Great wrote of it: "Nowhere do I feel as I do here. The sea air cures me of my health troubles better than any medicines. And I sleep better at my Monplaisir than anywhere. I dream of the sea and ships." Today the complex is one of "the most venerated relics of the nation's history".

The *Psyche* cloche fountain

Monplaisir became the first ever seaside palace in Russian architecture. Peter personally selected the site for its construction, himself drew up the plans for the building and gave it the name Monplaisir. The ensemble includes an attractive garden "in the Dutch taste" that was also designed by the Tsar. The centre of the garden is the *Sheaf* fountain with a powerful jet of water soaring up 4½ metres from its tufa base. The fountain embodied the power and wealth of the Russian Empire. The garden is also notable for the fact that eight oaks have survived here since the time of Catherine II, including one that was planted by the Empress herself. These are the oldest trees in the Lower Park.

The Grand Hall

The Monplaisir Palace

THE PALACE, a dainty single-storey building, was built by Peter I as a stylization of a wealthy Dutch house. Its appearance is an attractive mix of grandeur and simplicity, comfort and refinement. Thanks to the artificial embankment that Peter had constructed in front of the palace, Monplaisir acquired the look of a ship rushing into the sea. Here one senses best of all Peterhof's connection with the sea.

The Maritime Cabinet

The Secretary's Room

The middle part of the palace was constructed in 1714–16 (to a detailed plan believed to have been by Andreas Schlüter) and in the following two years it was extended with galleries and Lusthäuser (amusement pavilions). The interior decoration of the building was completed by 1723.

The interior layout of the palace, which Peter himself played a role in planning, is notable for its rationality. At the centre is the Grand Hall, adjoined on each side by three rooms: the Lacquer (Chinese) Cabinet, Kitchen and Pantry on the east; the Secretary's Room, Bedroom and Maritime Study on the west. The Grand Hall forms part of a suite comprising the Lusthäuser, galleries, the Lacquer Cabinet and the Secretary's Room.

Some of the outstanding specialists of the day worked on the decoration of the palace, including Jean-Baptiste Le Blond, Andreas Schlüter, Niccolo Michetti, Johann Friedrich Braunstein, Philippe Pillement, Nicolas Pineau, Jean Michel, Mikhail Negrubov, Alexander Zakharov and Perfily Fiodorov. Each interior is a unique cultural monument from the eighteenth century: the walls of the rooms are lined with oak "in the English manner"; the ceilings are decorated with stylish ornamental painting executed in tempera on plaster; the walls of the Kitchen and Bedroom are tiled; the floors in the central hall and in the gallery are paved with a chequered pattern of black and white marble.

The murals of Monplaisir (executed in tempera on dry plaster) are decorative-ornamental compositions with grotesque motifs on the theme of the seasons, human moods (smiling, frowning and playful-looking masks framed by scrolls), the gifts of nature (birds, fruit and flowers) and the elements (in the Grand Hall).

Monplaisir is also home to a rich collection of paintings by Western European artists of the late seventeenth and early eighteenth centuries – one of the first picture galleries in Russia. The foundation of this collection is made up of works by Dutch painters that Peter I purchased directly in the artists' studios during his visits to Holland (the first in 1697–98, as part of the Great Embassy, the second in 1716–1717).

The Lacquer Cabinet

The Catherine Block

THE CATHERINE BLOCK (originally the Elizabethan Block) was erected by Francesco Bartolomeo Rastrelli in the place of the old Monplaisir orangery. Construction was finished by 1748, but the decoration of the interiors dragged on for many years and was completed only by 1760. The internal layout of the block followed on the enfilade principle typical for Rastrelli, with the rooms connected directly with one another. The rooms are decorated with gilded carving, fabric wallpaper and parquet floors with chequered and zigzag patterns and lit by crystal chandeliers. In Empress Elizabeth's time the block was used for amusements, as a setting for small balls, concerts, masquerades and card-games.

In the summer of 1762, after Peter III came to the throne, the block — or more precisely the wooden "Tea-House" attached to it — was lived in by his estranged wife Catherine Alexeyevna until on 28 June she escaped to St Petersburg, where with the aid of members of the Guards she deposed her husband and was herself proclaimed empress.

The Green Reception Room

Oak chair with a lyre back. *Designed by Luigi Rusca. Russia. 1840s*

The Study of Alexander I

Rhyton goblet.
Two-layer glass,
bronze. Russia.
First quarter
of the 19th century

Clock with a figure
of Achilles.
Bronze. Made
by P.F. Foucher.
France. 1813—14

Porcelain vase.
Russia. Early
19th century

The Bedroom of Alexander I

The Yellow Hall ↪

In 1785–86, on Catherine II's orders, Giacomo Quarenghi aided by the sculptor Jacques-Dominique Rachette and the decorative artist Scotti completely remodelled the interiors of the block's eight rooms in the Classical style. The decoration made skilful use of one and the same approach: smooth walls of a single colour (blue, yellow or green) enlivened by pilasters, stucco-work and painting imitating reliefs. In 1810 the rooms were refurbished in the Empire style with the participation of the painter Giovanni Battista Scotti and given expensive furniture produced to the designs of major architects — Carlo Rossi, Andrei Voronikhin and Vasily Stasov — specially for Peterhof. Those were the last alterations in the block.

The Yellow Hall is the grandest room in the building. It contains a Gobelins tapestry that was commission by Napoleon based on a painting by Charles de Steuben showing Peter the Great rescuing fishermen during a storm on Lake Ladoga. The tapestry was completed

The Yellow Hall. Portrait of Empress Catherine II.
Early 19th century

Semicircular chest-of-drawers with a marquetry design worked in walnut, palisander and birch. *Made by Andrei Tur. Russia. 1848*

Porcelain vase. *Russia. First quarter of the 19th century*

Items from the Guryev Service

The Vestibule

after Napoleon's overthrow and Louis XVIII presented it to Alexander I. Alongside are portraits of Catherine II (an early nineteenth-century copy of the work by the Austrian Johann Baptist von Lampi the Elder) and Alexander I (1825, by George Dawe). On display here too is the Guryev Service, commissioned from the Imperial Porcelain Factory in 1809 when its director was Count Dmitry Guryev. Work on the service continued until the late nineteenth century and it is one of the world's largest (around 5,000 items) and most famous ensembles of porcelain.

The Blue Drawing-Room

The Bath and Kitchen Blocks

ADJOINING the Monplaisir palace on the east side is a complex of buildings created in the eighteenth and nineteenth centuries: the Bath Block, the Gentlemen's Bathhouse, the Assembly Room and the Kitchen Block, all tactfully incorporated into the Monplaisir ensemble. Today their interiors have been reconstructed and house some unique displays that present the everyday domestic side of palace life.

All the elements of the complex have their origins in service buildings from Peter's time when, in 1719–21, wooden guests' galleries were built onto Monplaisir on the east and west sides (architect: Johann Friedrich Braunstein) and at roughly the same time, in 1719–22, the architect Mikhail Zemtsov constructed by the eastern gallery a steam-bath in which iron cannonballs were used instead of the traditional stones on the stove. In 1726, under Catherine I, to the south of the bathhouse Zemtsov (assisted by others) began building kitchen premises and living quarters for the servants. That work was completed in 1732.

In 1743, in Empress Elizabeth's reign, the dilapidated bathhouse was replaced with a new one designed by Francesco Bartolomeo Rastrelli with a bathing pool and fountain. Between the Bathhouse and the Kitchens the architect inserted a wooden residential wing for the Empress's entourage that compositionally united all the buildings.

Ladies' linen from the Steam Room

The Steam Room

The Cold Bathroom

The Warm Bathroom. A Bacchante Resting.
Artist: Nikanor Tiutriumov. 1867

family used the Monplaisir steam-bath. That is why in 1866 in place of the decayed Rastrelli wing for the entourage Eduard Hahn built a masonry Bath Block in which a set of sitting and bathing rooms were created for Empress Maria Alexandrovna, the wife of Alexander II. The architect decorated the exterior of the block in the style of Peter the Great's time — a mansard roof, rusticated decorative elements, small-paned windows and painting in three colours.

The Dressing Room

In 1800, under Paul I, a masonry bathhouse designed by Giacomo Quarenghi took the place of the wooden one. In the nineteenth century a steam-bath for ladies and gentlemen was added to it.

In Nicholas I's reign special rooms began to be set aside in the palaces of Peterhof for baths and showers. There were such rooms in the Cottage palace in Alexandria. Despite that, the imperial

The table laid in the Assembly Hall

The Assembly Hall. The *America* tapestry

Chair. *Russia*.
1720s

The Assembly Hall is the most attractive interior in the complex. It is located beneath the same roof as the rooms of the Kitchen Block.

They can all trace their history back to 2 September 1725, when Catherine I gave orders "to build by Monplaisir kitchen chambers and other rooms in accordance with the drawing made by the architect Zemtsov." On 16 November 1747 her daughter Elizabeth ordered the architect Rastrelli to produce designs for the conversion of the kitchen at Monplaisir into living rooms. To turn the kitchen premises of Catherine I's time into a grand Assembly Hall the number of windows was increased and a new entrance from the Monplaisir garden created. The walls were panelled with oak and decorated with 17 tapestries woven at the St Petersburg factory in the first half of the eighteenth century. The Russian-made chairs from the 1720s are also upholstered with tapestries. In the mid-1700s this place was known as "the hall where the gentlemen dine" or the "Moorish Hall" (due to the African theme of the tapestries). In the eighteenth and nineteenth centuries it was used as a banquet hall.

From the Assembly Hall doors lead into the first room of the Kitchen Block — the Pantry, a fairly small interior with a vaulted ceiling that was used for storing table linen and items for laying and decorating banquet tables. The wooden cupboards running the length of the walls have been recreated from Rastrelli's drawing. The Pantry is connected to a spacious

The Kitchen

Kitchen with a splendid view of the Lower Park through its windows. The kitchen created to Rastrelli's design was still in use in the early twentieth century. The interiors of the Kitchen Block end with the Coffee Pantry, a tribute to the new eighteenth-century court fashion of drinking coffee that was introduced to Russia by Peter the Great. On display here are splendid coffee and tea services, a collection of samovars, a brazier from the second half of the nineteenth century, coffee-grinders, coffee-makers and other items.

View of the Bathhouse Block from the Ménager Fountain in the Chinese Garden

The Chinese Garden

THIS SMALL gem of a garden with winding paths was laid out in the 1860s on the east side of the Bath Block by the master gardener Balthasar following the design of the architect Eduard Hahn. In its layout Hahn employed compositional devices found in Chinese and Japanese landscape art. Everything here is miniature and exquisite — the tufa grotto with a *Seashell* cascade, the *Vase* fountain, the picturesque pool, the little humpback bridges over the stream, the irregularly-shaped flowerbeds. The garden also has some marble sculpture — *Antinous* and *Cupid and Psyche*. In the south-west corner of the garden the makers created a "Mount Parnassus", a small elevation that provides an enchanting view of the Gulf of Finland.

From the Chinese Garden you can see that another building, red-brick with a hipped roof adjoins the Bath Block at an angle. This is the Gentlemen's Steam-Bath — successor to the first bathhouse of Peter's time that was rebuilt in masonry by Quarenghi in 1800 on Paul I's orders. In 1865–66 Hahn reworked its facades to match the style of Monplaisir.

The layout inside has come down to us without any substantial alterations. Today visitors can enjoy its restored interiors including the Guest Room from the Service Wing of Peter I's day that is connected to the bathhouse, a room for servants and for heating water where various old bathing utensils are on display, the Gentlemen's Room where male toilet articles from the eighteenth century and first half of the nineteenth are on show, the Bathroom for Maids-of-Honour with a collection of bathtubs, and other rooms with a practical purpose.

The *Seashell* Cascade in the Chinese Garden

The Sea Canal

THE SEA CANAL forms the central axis of the Lower Park, dividing it into two parts – east and west. Little bridges carry the Marly and Maliban Alleys across the canal. From the central bridge there are striking views southwards to the Great Palace and Great Cascade and northwards to the sea, which gives Peterhof a special charm. The canal is 12 metres wide, around 500 metres long and up to 3 metres deep. Its construction began in January 1716 and ended by the summer of 1721. Originally it was navigable, but in 1735 with the installation of the Samson fountain

in the basin, vessels stopped going up to the palace. Only on festive occasions did yachts enter the canal to provide illuminations. The fountain adornment of the Sea Canal changed several times. Today it comprises 22 round basins with jets that rise to a height of six metres, resembling the slender trunks of fabulous crystal trees. This similarity led to this ensemble becoming known as the Alley of Fountains.

The Adam and Eve Fountains

FROM MONPLAISIR two paths to the south-west return visitors to the Marly Alley, reaching it at the site of the *Adam* fountain, one of the oldest at Peterhof. It is one of a pair, with *Eve* that also stands on the Marly Alley in the western part of the Lower Park.

Installation of the two fountains began in 1720 and they were intended to symbolize the union in marriage of Peter I and Catherine I. Their locations at the crossing points of alleys on the east and west sides of the Lower Park an equal distance from the Sea Canal make the fountains nodal points in the composition of the park.

The marble sculptures of Adam and Eve were made in Venice to a commission from Peter I by the sculptor Giovanni Bonazza in 1717. They are free copies of famous works by Antonio Rizzi that adorn the Palace of the Doges in Venice. They were set in the centre of identical 17-metre-diameter octagonal basins. From the base of each of the pedestals sixteen jets spurt to a height of 6½ metres, forming a crown-like decoration of water.

Adam was put into operation first, during Peter's lifetime. The *Eve* fountain, created by Timofei Usov to the same design on the orders of Catherine I, was inaugurated in 1726.

The decorative setting for the fountains includes trellised pavilions. The first summerhouses appeared here back in Peter's time and were designed by the architect Michetti. Over the years their number and appearance changed several times.

The Hermitage Pavilion

THE HERMITAGE PAVILION, approached by the radial paths running north-westwards from the *Eve* fountain, is "a little architectural pearl" of Peterhof, a favourite place for royal amusements. This was the first "hermitage" in Russia, constructed in imitation of French prototypes that were very popular in the seventeenth and eighteenth centuries. Such miniature palatial "places of solitude" were a typical attribute of French regular gardens in that period and were intended as a place for the owners to spend leisure hours with a small circle of friends.

The history of Peterhof's Hermitage goes back to Peter I's decree dated January 1721 "at Peterhof in the coming summer another Monplaisir is to be made..." Construction began that year to a design by Johann Friedrich Braunstein and was completed in the summer of 1725, by which time Peter had died. On 25 July 1725 his widow and successor, Catherine I, visited "the new house in the Peterhof garden that is called the Hermitage".

Like Monplaisir, this pavilion stands right on the seashore and it is at the end of the western radial alley running from the Great Palace. The building is surrounded by a moat and is attractive for the fine proportions of its architecture and refined decoration. The pavilion is rendered particularly stylish by the wrought-iron work on the windows

The Kitchen

The lift mechanism

The Pavilion Hall (State Dining-Room)

and balconies that is painted black with gilded details. On Peter's orders the oak balconies were made like on his ship, the *Ingermanlandia*. The scrolled oak brackets that support them were decorated with carving designed by Nicolas Pineau.

Inside the Hermitage Peter had a special lifting mechanism made. On the upper storey a large oval table for 14 diners was installed with a central section that could be lowered to the floor below, laid with dishes and sent back up. There were also smaller round "place mats" raised and lowered on rods. Each guest could order a separate dish by placing a note on a plate and pulling a ring connected to a string that rang a bell in the Pantry downstairs. This "curiosity" was lost during the war, but after 65 long years it was restored in 2009.

The Hermitage's painting collection, begun with pictures purchased by Peter the Great, numbers 124 canvases. It includes *The Battle of Poltava* by an unknown Russian artist and works by Western European artists of the seventeenth and eighteenth centuries.

The Battle of Poltava. *Copy by an unknown 18th-century artist of a 1727 painting by Ivan Nikitin*

The Lion Cascade

FROM THE MAIN façade of the Hermitage a path leads
to the *Lion Cascade* – a magnificent Ionic colonnade
in the centre of a basin. Within the colonnade there
are a dozen white marble bowls from which tall jets
of water spurt. Around the edge of the plinth bronze
masks spit water into the basin. In the centre
of the colonnade is a fountain featuring a sculpture
of Aganippe, the naiad or nymph of a spring at
the foot of Mount Helicon, by the eminent Russian
sculptor Fiodor Tolstoi. On the north side in front
of the colonnade stand bronze lions spouting water.
They were cast from a model by Ivan Prokofiev.

The present colonnade, whose dark granite
contrasts beautifully with the white Carrara marble
used for the architrave and the capitals and bases
of the columns, was erected on the spot where
as early as 1800 the architect Andrei Voronikhin
created the Hermitage Cascade (named after
the nearby pavilion). In the 1850s that installation
was dismantled to be replaced by a new one
designed by Andrei Stakenschneider, which has
become known as the *Lion Cascade*. Work on it was
completed by June 1857.

The Memorial Bench

A LITTLE to the north of the *Lion Cascade*, in the shade
of the trees, there stands one more object designed by the
architect Stakenschneider. This is a memorial bench set up
in remembrance of the youngest daughter of Nicholas I,
Alexandra Nikolayevna. She married the Prince of Hesse-
Kassel in Germany, but died aged just 19 at Tsarskoye Selo
on 29 July 1844.

The bench was created in 1844–45 in the marble
workshop run in St Petersburg by Alessandro Triscorni.
It is topped by a bust of Alexandra Nikolayevna by the
sculptor Ivan Vitali.

The Marly Ensemble

THIS SPLENDID creation of Peter I's time is located at the western end of the Lower Park. It takes the form of a regular garden with an area of 12.5 hectares protected from the Gulf by a tall man-made embankment and on the south by the natural terrace, down which the Golden Hill cascade descends. The centre of the ensemble is an exquisite palace erected

A monument to Peter I holding the 7-year-old King Louis XV of France in his arms

on the strip of land between two ponds. The appearance of the palace has remained unchanged since its completion.
The ensemble was given the name Marly in memory of the French royal residence of Marly-le-Roi, which Peter the Great visited
in 1717 during his second journey abroad. The Tsar spent five days there, from 27 to 31 May, during which time he celebrated
his birthday. However, the name Marly appeared in Peterhof's official documents not on its founder's initiative, but only
in the middle of the eighteenth century.

The Marly Palace

THE PLAN for the "Small Seaside Chambers", as the Marly palace is called in the documents of Peter's time, was drawn up by the architect Johann Friedrich Braunstein in accordance with the main principles of *A Project for a Model Country Estate* by Domenico Trezzini.

Construction work began in 1720. In the original concept the palace was to be a single-storey building, but when roofing began, Peter gave orders for a second floor to be added as it became clear that it was out of proportion with the size of the Great Pond. By 1725 construction was complete.

The seemingly miniature palace with an almost square ground-plan and cubic volume is topped by a mansard roof that has fanciful lines typical for the period (a similar shape could be seen in the roof of the Monbijou palace outside

The Kitchen

European-made table ware. *18th century*

The Vestibule

Berlin, on account of which the Marly was sometimes called "Monbijou").

The decoration of the facades is extremely simple — only the balconies stand out with their sculpted brackets and wrought-iron railings where gold scrolls glitter among the black curves.

The decoration of the palace was the work of the master masons A. Cardasier and Yakov Neupokoyev, the smith G. Belin (wrought-iron on the balconies and oak staircase), the decorative sculptor N. Pineau (designs for the embellishments of the

Long-case clock.
Made by Willem Koster. Holland.
First third of the 18th century

The Pantry. Delftware, Chinese and Japanese porcelain. *17th – early 18th centuries*

Chair with marquetry decoration. *Holland. Early 18th century*

The Dining-Room

balcony and stair railings, the Oak Study), the master joiner J. Michel (Oak Staircase, Plane-Tree Study, balcony brackets), the stucco-artists Rossi and Quadri (bas-reliefs, Entrance Hall) and Russian specialists — masons, moulders and plasterers, parquet-makers.

As early as the mid-eighteenth century the palace had acquired the status of a house-museum, in which a unique collection of the first Russian emperor's personal belongings had been assembled. In 1918 the palace was turned into a museum of history and daily life with over 300 exhibits.

Inside the Marly Palace is simple and comfortable. It has sixteen rooms none of which were exclusively used as grand state rooms. The most elegant are the Vestibule, the Dining-Room, the Oak and Plane-Tree Studies, and the Bedroom (lined with a fabric that has a fine pattern of carnations and chamomiles. Hanging in all the rooms are paintings from Peter's collection. The palace also boasts attractive well-made furniture, porcelain items that were very precious at that time, Chinese enamels, a Dutch long-case clock and more, including still some of Peter's authentic belongings.

The palace also has a library — a small and modestly finished room that houses some unique publications from the eighteenth century.

Display case with a collection of Chinese enamels.
Holland. First half of the 18th century

Figure of a dog. *China. 18th century*

The Bedroom

View of the Marly Park from the Golden Hill cascade ↳

The Library   The Oak Study

The Golden Hill Cascade Ensemble

THE GOLDEN HILL cascade and the parterre in front of it is the most impressive part of the Marly ensemble. Construction of the cascade began in 1721 to the design of Niccolo Michetti with the participation of the sculptor Bartolomeo Carlo Rastrelli. In 1724 direction of the project passed to Mikhail Zemtsov, who completed it by 1732. It was this architect who had the steps of the cascade faced with sheets of gilded copper.

The water is disgorged onto the cascade from three gilded masks on the upper wall that were made by Bartolomeo Carlo Rastrelli to sketches by Michetti. Rising from the parterre at the foot of the cascade are the jets of the mighty *Ménager Fountains* whose effect comes solely from the force and (15-metre) height of their foaming columns. These were designed by Peter I himself. The opening of the pipe is almost closed off by a cone inserted into it, leaving just a narrow ring-shaped aperture through which the water emerges forming a column that is 30 centimetres wide but hollow inside. This creates an impression of unparalleled power while using relatively little water. As a result the installation became known as the *Ménager Fountains* from the French word for "economize". Next to them are four miniature fountains from the eighteenth century decorated with figures of Tritons who hold above their heads bells (cloches) over which the water descends.

The white marble sculpture of the cascade

The Medici Venus in the Garden of Ve
18th century. The Ménager Fountains

One of the *Triton* fountains
in the Garden of Bacchus

The houses for maids-of-honour.
Artist: Alexander Benois. 1900

THE MUSEUMS
OF PETERHOF

THE NEW museums in Peterhof offer unique thematic collections displayed in restored historical buildings from the nineteenth century situated in the Lower Park, the Upper Garden and the Palace Square.

The creation of these museums was prompted by the need to present more fully and broadly the history of Peterhof as a summer imperial residence — a history that was not limited to court festivities and grand ceremonial events, but also includes a host of highly interesting details that unfold before us in a broad and many-sided picture of daily life at Peterhof. The establishment of museums dedicated to separate aspects of life in the residence became possible thanks to collections donated to the Peterhof State Museum Preserve and the numerous acquisitions that have been made in recent decades.

Today there are six of these thematic museums: (1) The Imperial Yachts; (2) The Museum of Imperial Bicycles; (3) The Museum of Fountain-Making; (4) The Museum of the Benois Family; (5) The Museum of Collectors and (6) The Museum of Playing Cards.

Panorama of the Upper Garden
with Olga's Pond in the foreground

Peter the Great's yacht sailing off the Dutch coast. *Artist: Abraham Storck. 1690–1710*

The Imperial Yachts Museum

BY PETERHOF'S little dock there is a small building that houses the Imperial Yachts Museum, which tells its visitors about a little-known chapter in the history of Peterhof as the base of the fleet of imperial yachts. Here, at the summer residence of the Russian rulers, there was a special harbour for the moorage of the imperial yachts that for more than 200 years were on the rolls of the Russian navy.

On show in the museum are models of the yachts that were truly "floating imperial residences", unique objects of daily use at sea including collections of imperial yacht table services, paintings, works of graphic art

The museum building

A model of the sno
Munker made by t
marine engineer Vic
Krainiukov. *2003*

Plaque: Emperor Nicholas I's Visit to England in 1844.
Painting by A. Meshchersky after a painting by Nicholas Matthew Condy the Younger. 1855—81. Imperial Porcelain Factory, St Petersburg

The Imperial Yacht *Derzhava* in the Open Sea.
Artist: A. Bobrov. 1901

Items from the formal table service of the yacht *Livadia*.
Designed by Ippolito Monighetti. 1871—73

and historical photographs depicting the imperial yachts. The display is spread over three halls. The first contains exhibits relating to the history of imperial yachts in the eighteenth century: a model of the snow *Munker* that is connected with the first-ever mention of Peterhof; copies of Peter I's seaman's jacket and naval greatcoat and Catherine II uniform-style dress (the originals are in the stocks of the Peterhof Museum Preserve) and more. There are portraits too, including one of Paul I, who in December 1762, at the age of 8, was appointed admiral general of the Russian Navy by his Empress mother.

The second hall presents the history of the imperial yachts *Victoria, Derzhava, Alexandria, Livadia, Poliarnaya Zvezda, Strelna, Nixa, Slavianka, Marevo, Tsarevna* and others.

The third hall is entirely devoted to the *Shtandart*, the favourite yacht of Nicholas II's family. It was built at Copenhagen in 1896 and named in honour of the 28-gun frigate that Peter the Great built at the Olonets shipyard in 1703. The last Russian emperor's best memories were connected with the *Shtandart*.

Emperor Nicholas II's family aboard the yacht
Shtandart. 1906 photograph

THE CZAR AND FAMILY.
PRINCESS OLGA.   CZAR NICHOLAS II.   PRINCESS ANASTAZIA.   CZARINA ALEXANDRA FEODOROVNA.   PRINCESS TATIANA
CZAREWITCH ALEXIS.   PRINCESS MARIE   ROTARY PHO

Child's bicycle. *Coventry, England. 1880s*   Child's tricycle. *France. 1870s*

The Museum of Imperial Bicycles

THIS MUSEUM, located in one of the houses built to accommodate the gentlemen of the court in the late eighteenth century (architect: Franz Brouer), illustrates one of the most fascinating aspects of the private life outside the capital of the Russian monarchs who were very fond of technical innovations.

The first bicycle resembling those we know today was put together in 1863 by the 19-year-old Frenchman Pierre Lallement. The following year the Olivier brothers, entrepreneurs with a base in Lyons, recognized the potential of the invention and soon began mass production of bicycles with a metal frame devised by the carriage-maker Pierre Michaux. And as early as 1867 the first bicycle made its appearance at the Russian court.

The museum display spread over six halls makes it possible to trace the story of the creation and evolution of the bicycle. It contains a dozen different pedal-driven vehicles that belonged to the Russian emperors and their children — from the early "boneshaker" made in Paris in 1867 for Emperor Alexander II to a tricycle made in England in the late nineteenth century that belonged to Tsesarevich Alexei. Here too are the famous "penny-farthing" or high-wheeler, a tandem "bicycle made for two", and the childhood bicycles of grand dukes and duchesses.

The museum building

Child's bicycle. *Russia. 1870s*

Rudge tricycle.
England. 1883

Tricycle. *England. 1880.*
Belonged to the future Nicholas II

Visitors are helped to sense the spirit of an era when the cycling craze gripped the whole of Russian society by posters, photographs and postcards.

Rudge-Whitworth lady's tricycle.
England. 1908. Belonged to Tsesarevich Alexei

"Penny-farthing" bicycle made by the Premier Cycle Company, Ltd, England. *1882. Belonged to Alexander III*

Tsesarevich Alexei, Nicholas II's only son. *1913 photograph*

The display also includes rare postage stamps, playing cards, cuff-links, medals and other items that feature the image of a cyclist, old bicycle number plates, bells, a variety of lamps and other cycling accessories of the early years.

The Museum of Fountain-Making

THIS MUSEUM, which opened in 2004, presents the history of one of the most important components of the Peterhof ensemble – its unique fountain system.

It is located in Peterhof's *Delovoi Dvor* – a complex that contained a number of workshops (metalworking, woodworking, soldering, fountain-engineering and so on). It was here that equipment for the Peterhof fountains was created and preparatory work for their maintenance was carried out.

It is obvious that the Peterhof fountains are not only a magnificent spectacle, but also a tremendous hydraulic complex that comprises 135 engineering structures, including 39 bridges, 28 pipe crossings, 33 sluices and other elements. Around 30 kilometres of buried pipes run through the Upper Garden and Lower Park. The total length of the water channels is 56 kilometres.

The museum's exhibits provide a detailed introduction to all these components. They include old plans, among them a unique one (the original is in the National Museum in Stockholm) copied by J. Rindahl in 1739 from a diagram made by Michetti in 1722.

A special place in the display is taken by examples of eighteenth-century pipes. In Peter I's time the water was delivered to the fountains mainly through cast-iron pipes.

Plan of the Great Cascade
"showing the water supply pipes". *1824*

Mask from a Roman Fountain. *After a model by Ivan Martos*

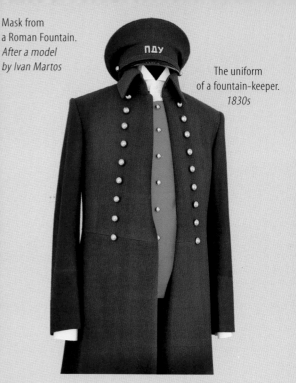

The uniform of a fountain-keeper. *1830s*

Today as in the eighteenth century the pipes that branch off from the mains to take the water the last stage to the fountain jets are made of lead.

Among the extremely interesting exhibits are models of sculptural fountain groups, firework figures, examples of fountain nozzles and lampions used for illuminations during festivities in Peter I's time by placing them around the edge of the fountain basins.

There is also material on the history of the Ropsha canal, costumes worn by the fountain maintenance crew in the 1830s and much else.

Three-bar wheel, one of the models of figures for firework displays. *20th century*

A machine for boring pipes. Recreated from early 18th-century drawings by Andrei Nartov

The Benois Family Museum

OPENED IN 1988 on the initiative of Nikolai Alexandrovich Benois, for many years the chief designer at La Scala theatre in Milan, this museum is devoted to a famous dynasty of architects, artists, sculptors and musicians who have played a considerable role in the history of Peterhof.

The display includes some 800 works of painting, sculpture and graphic art, examples of theatrical decorative art, architectural projects, rare photographs and authentic items that belonged to the most distinguished of the Benois clan.

The founder of the dynasty was Louis Jules Auguste César Benois. He was considered one of the finest cooks in Paris and that brought him an invitation to become court chef to Paul I. His middle son, Nikolai Benois, became a prominent court architect. It is from his collection that one of the gems of the Hermitage picture gallery comes – the *Benois Madonna* by Leonardo da Vinci. He was also the creator of a number of architectural

Portrait of Nikolai Benois
by Victor Dumitrashko. *1901*

The museum building

The Benois family tree. *1894*

Portrait of Maria Pavlova-Benois
by Zinaida Serebriakova. *1923*

monuments in Peterhof, including the court stables in Gothic style, the railway station commissioned by Baron Stieglitz, the owner of the line, and the building that now houses the museum — formerly an accommodation block for maids-of-honour.

Nikolai Benois was the father of the architect Leonty Benois, the watercolour artist Albert Benois and one of the foremost figures of Russia's "Silver Age" in the early 1900s — the artist and art theorist Alexander Benois, one of the founders of the World of Art grouping and a close associate of Sergei Diaghilev in organizing the famous *Ballets Russes* tours abroad. Part of the display is devoted to the creative works of the Lanceray family, one of the branches of the Benois. They included the sculptor Yevgeny Lanceray (grandson of a captured Napoleonic officer), his sons, the artist Yevgeny and the architect Nikolai, and also his daughter, the outstanding artist Zinaida Serebriakova. The display includes works by other members of the Benois and Lanceray lines, including those who lived in emigration.

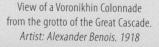

View of a Voronikhin Colonnade
from the grotto of the Great Cascade.
Artist: Alexander Benois. 1918

Illustration for Sir Walter Scott's novel *Quentin Durward*.
Artist: Alexander Benois. 1890

The Museum of Collectors

THE DISPLAY of the Museum of Collectors is situated in eight rooms of the Upper Garden House that was built to Nikolai Benois's design in 1861–68. The museum opened in the summer of 2002 with stocks formed from two private collections.

The history of the collection belonging to Iosif Ezrakh — one of the best known Leningrad-Petersburg collectors in the twentieth century — began in 1927 with the purchase of some Saxon porcelain items at an auction held in Apraxin Dvor, where at that time there were regular sales of items from the requisitioned homes of the old St Petersburg nobility. Today the Peterhof Museum Preserve has 800 items collected by Ezrakh. They include very rare eighteenth-century snuffboxes, bonbonnières and beauty-spot boxes, Russian and European porcelain of the eighteenth to twentieth centuries and works by prominent Russian artist of the early 1900s — Petrov-Vodkin, Falk, Saryan, Dobuzhinsky, Lebedev, Larionv, Serebriakova and others.

Clock.
Made in France.
Second half
of the 18th
century

The museum building

Dish: Harlequinade. *Design by V. Mosiagin. 1922. Former Imperial Porcelain Factory, Petrograd*

The collection of Roza and Alexander Timofeyev consists of eighty works of painting and graphic art and over 2,500 books and periodicals, including publications illustrated by Ivan Bilibin, Vladimir Konashevich and Sergei Chekhonin. A section apart is formed by a superb collection of sixteenth- to nineteenth-century drawings that was put together by Vladimir Kurbatov and acquired by the Timofeyevs. The couple's collection is also the source for works of "agitation porcelain" and works of art by Alexander Benois, David Burliuk, Yevgeny Lanceray , Boris Kustodiev and Mikhail Nesterov.

Porcelain figurine: Gardener. *Modelled by Michel Victor Acier. Meissen, Germany. Circa 1777*

Katiusha on a Blanket. *Artist: Zinaida Serebriakova. 1920s*

Portrait of the actress Anna Heinz by Vasily Shukhayev. *1916—17*

Fruit. *Artist: Pavel Kuznetsov. 1919*

RSFSR plate. *Design by P. Vychegzhanin. 1920. Former Imperial Porcelain Factory, Petrograd*

The Museum of Playing Cards

THE MUSEUM'S display has been open to the public since 2007 in one of the houses for gentlemen of the court at Peterhof that were built in 1798–99 by the architect Franz Brouer. Here the collection of Alexander Perelman, that the Peterhof Museum Preserve acquired in 1999, is used as basis to present the whole history of playing cards in the East, Europe, Russia and America.

It is no coincidence that the museum appeared in Peterhof: it was here in summer that a select society would gather for lunch and dinner parties, masquerades and court balls. At the balls they would not only dance but also play cards.

Besides Peterhof in Russia there are three museum collections of playing-cards belonging to the Hermitage, the State Historical Museum in Moscow and the Ivanovo Regional Art Museum. But the Peterhof museum is the first and only specialist museum in the country devoted to playing cards.

In its six halls more than 8,000 exhibits are on display. Apart from cards and items reflecting their history, there are also collections of ex libris, numismatics, examples of dice and descriptions of games played by many peoples and countries and also playing equipment and accessories.

Fortune-telling cards: The Russian Soothsayer. *Artist: Nikolai Petrov. 1911*

Historical playing cards.
Artist: N. Karazin.
Second half of the
19th century

Anti-Fascist
playing cards.
Artist: Vasily Vlasov.
1941

карты
ИТАЛЬЯНСКИЕ

из собрания ГМЗ "Петергоф"

Pack of musical cards for the game
of trapola

Playing cards with a military theme.
St Petersburg. 1880—90

One of the halls is devoted to the famous Tarot cards and various gambling games popular in Europe.
The museum also has a fortune-telling hall that presents various methods of predicting the future and another
devoted to the history of playing cards in Russia. Visitors also learn about artists who applied their skills to designing
cards and about the history of gambling in Russian literature.

New Figures playing cards.
Artist: Adolphe Charlemagne. 1860s

Travelling playing cards.
Artist: Adolphe Charlemagne. 1860s

The Card Joke
transformation
playing cards.
Artist: Johann
Caspar Beeg.
Germany

THE COLONISTS' PARK

THE PARK is a monument of Peterhof in the time of Nicholas I, who was especially fond of this imperial summer residence. His wife, Alexandra Fiodorovna, was also enchanted with Peterhof and her husband made her a gift of large expanses of land to the east and south of the main ensemble dating back to Peter I's reign.

The Colonists' Park was laid out to the design of Andrei Stakenschneider under the direction of the master landscape gardener Peter Ehrler to the south of the Upper Garden, in place of the huge Hunting Marsh. It got its name from the houses of German settlers or "colonists" located here. Work on creating the ensemble was complete by 1857. The greater part of the 29-hectare territory is occupied by the picturesque Olga's Pond, named in honour of one of Nicholas I's daughters. On two fairly small islands in the pond two fairly small pavilions were erected — the Tsarina's and Olga's. The islands could only be reached by ferry, or else by rowing boat or gondola, which gave them a special romantic air. The Tsarina's Pavilion, which belonged to Empress Alexandra Fiodorovna, was the first to be built.

The Cathedral of SS Peter and Paul in the Colonists' Park.
Architect: Nikolai Sultanov. 1905.
The Tsarina's Pavilion

133

The Tsarina's Pavilion

THE MINIATURE single-storey pavilion in the Pompeian style with a three-storey tower was begun in 1842. It stands on the very edge of the lake. In front of its southern façade there is a parterre with a Carrara marble fountain basin in the centre containing a statue of Narcissus (1846; sculptor: Konstantin Klimchenko). On the north side the pavilion is adjoined by the Private Garden, where neat flowerbeds effectively set off classically-shaped marble vases, capitals, and a limestone bench with a Carrara marble bust of Diana (1842). The garden's most romantic adornment is a glass column set up here in 1854. It was a gift to Alexandra Fiodorovna from her brother, King Frederick William IV of Prussia. The column is topped by a gilded sculpture of *A Girl Feeding a Parrot with Grapes* (from a model by the Berlin sculptor Heinrich Berges).

The interior of the pavilion is astonishing for its infinite refinement. The central space is the Atrium – an imitation of an Ancient Roman courtyard. In the centre of the Atrium Stakenschneider placed a square pool (*impluvium*) faced with different-coloured marbles and containing a fountain. The interior is painted in the "Pompeian" style and richly embellished with marble.

The Oikos (Drawing-Room)

The Inner Courtyard

Connected to the Atrium is an Exedra (a room with niches) that was an invariable feature of a wealthy Pompeian house. Here it is a square room with marble floors embellished with three niches topped with conches that are painted in imitation of coffering. All the fittings and furnishings were executed by Russian and French craftsmen in the "Pompeian" style.

The second room adjoining the Atrium is the Oikos (living room) where again marbles of various shades play the leading role in the decoration. The windows of the Oikos look out onto a terrace enclosed by a trellis-like cast-iron grille and adorned by a figure of a *Sleeping Nymph*.

In the sumptuously finished Dining-Room the floor is decorated with a rare genuine Ancient Roman mosaic measuring 3.7 metres square that Nicholas I acquired from Duke Maximilian of Leuchtenberg, the husband of his eldest daughter, Grand Duchess Maria Nikolayevna. On display here are items from the splendid Coral and Etruscan services that were made specially for the Tsarina's Pavilion at the Imperial Porcelain Factory.

One more room in the pavilion – Alexandra Fiodorovna's Study – is remarkable for the two Byzantine columns (twelfth–fifteenth centuries) that were used in its decoration. A door from the study leads to an inner courtyard where there are steps to the second floor of the tower, which contains the Emperor's Study. The courtyard itself is adorned with sculpture and fountains.

One of the three niches
of the Exedra

The Dining-Room

Olga's Island and Pavilion

OLGA'S PAVILION was a wedding gift from Nicholas I to his daughter, Olga, on her marriage to the Prince of Württemberg.

The story of the pavilion's construction begins with the purchase of the island by the imperial treasury on 23 June 1845. By spring the following year landscaping and improvement work had been carried out: demolition of old buildings, reinforcing the shore line, laying out flowerbeds and planting trees and shrubs under the direction of Peter Ehrler. On 29 March 1846 the architect Andrei Stakenschneider received the Emperor's approval, sent from Palermo, for his plan for a pavilion on Olga's Island with the instructions "immediately set about building the little house in the Italian style on Olga's Island." Just two months were allotted for the construction of the pavilion.

Olga Nikolayevna's Study

Nicholas I's Study

Nicholas I

On 1 June 1846 the building was completed in the rough, but finishing work continued until 1848.

In style Olga's Pavilion resembles the villas on the outskirts of Palermo, at one of which the Russian imperial family stayed in 1846. Therefore it is a sort of "reminiscence of Palermo", a place of warmth, calm and contemplation.

Terraces, balconies, a loggia, wooden pergolas, bas-reliefs, busts in niches and original water spouts in the form of winged dragons make the building exceptionally picturesque. Inside the pavilion has one room on each of the three floors (Dining-Room, Olga Nikolayevna's Study, Nicholas I's Study) decorated in a modest but refined manner. A viewing platform was created on the roof of the building, giving a splendid panorama of Peterhof and its surroundings. From here Nicholas I was even able to watch naval manoeuvres taking place in Kronstadt harbour.

Table in Olga Nikolayevna's Study

THE ALEXANDRIA PARK

ALEXANDRIA is an extensive (115-hectare, 280-acre) landscape park to the east of the Lower Park. It occupies the territory that in Peter I's time belonged to Prince Menshikov's estate Moncourage. Later there were imperial hunting grounds here that became the property of Grand Duke Nicholas (the future Nicholas I).

The creation of the now famous ensemble began in the year 1826 when, almost immediately after his succession to the throne (in December 1825), Nicholas gave orders for the construction here of "a country house or so-called 'cotich' with all utilities in combination with a park". The Emperor presented the estate to his wife, Alexandra Fiodorovna, in whose honour it was given the name "Her Majesty's Own Dacha Alexandria". The work on Alexandria was directed by the architect Adam Menelaws, who in collaboration with the master gardeners Friedrich Wendelsdorf and Peter Ehrler created by 1831 a splendid landscape park in the English style. The Cottage is the chief building in the park that also contains the Farm Palace and the Church of Alexander Nevsky (the Gothic Chapel).

The Cottage Palace

The Cottage Palace

THIS PALACE was constructed in 1826—29 to Menelaws's design, patterned on English country houses. The finishing touches to its architecture were made in 1842—43 by Andrei Stakenschneider, who added on the east side the Dining-Room and a marble terrace with a fountain. It was at that time too that a white marble *Madonna and Child* by Ivan Vitali was installed in a niche by the terrace.

Inside the Cottage is a surprising combination of elegant luxury and cosiness. There are no sumptuous state rooms here due to the private character of the palace. Carved wooden panels and stuccowork played an enormous role in the decoration of the rooms.

On the ground floor of the Cottage were Alexandra Fiodorovna's rooms and those for general use; on the floor above the rooms of Nicholas I and the children and at the top the rooms of the courtiers in attendance. A cast-iron staircase leads from the miniature Vestibule decorated with characteristic Gothic ornaments to the upper floors. The absence of additional supports, something new in palace construction at that time, enabled the architect to make the stairs seem almost weightless.

On the wall of the Vestibule before the staircase hangs a shield made from the shell of a sea-turtle bearing with

The Library

140

the arms of Alexandria — a sword passing through a wreath of white roses on a blue ground and the motto *For Faith, Tsar and Country*. The design was invented by the poet Vasily Zhukovsky and approved on 24 December 1829.

The suite of Alexandra Fiodorovna's rooms begins with her study, where every last detail was made in the Neo-Gothic style: the stucco ornament on the ceiling, the painting of the stove resembling the tracery of Gothic windows, and so on. Gothic motifs — spires, finials, turrets, lancet arches and little pyramids were also used to decorate the furniture and chandeliers.

After the Study comes the Drawing-Room, the central room of the ground floor, its layout, decoration and furnishings all show an obvious striving after an organic unity between the indoor space and the environment beyond. The huge windows of the bay and the glazed terrace doors connect the interior with the park. The main motif of the carving on the window and door surrounds is a grapevine. Plant motifs are also present in the decoration of the marble fireplaces that were made in Alessandro Triscorni's workshop.

Alexandra Fiodorovna's Study

Rose clock. *Metal and mother-of-pearl. Western Europe. First half of the 19th century*

The Dining-Room

Maria Fiodorovna's Study

The next room in the suite is the Library with Russian-made mahogany furniture from the 1830s. Then comes the Large Reception Room, the intimate size of which is proof that there were no large receptions at the Cottage: in the second quarter of the nineteenth century the private life of the imperial family became separated from the official one and any sort of substantial receptions, banquets or other festivities were held in the Great Palace at Peterhof. On the walls here are landscapes by Silvester Shchedrin, Maxim Vorobyev and Ivan Aivazovsky and a very rare work in the genre by the outstanding portraitist Orest Kiprensky – *A View of Vesuvius*.

The Dining-Room, decorated with wood panelling carved with Gothic ornament, is located in the extension that Stakenschneider built onto the palace in 1842. It is connected to the older part of the building by an effective lancet arcade. The furnishings consist of tables and oak chairs with high carved backs. On the tables are remarkable services featuring Gothic decoration and the arms of Alexandria. Here too there are items made in Bohemia, Russia, Silesia, Italy and France from brightly coloured glass (ruby, cobalt, pink, yellow and more). Like the previous room the Dining-Room is hung with painting, including five by the eminent seascape-painter Ivan Aivazovsky.

One further room on the ground floor – the Small Reception Room (used by maids-of-honour in attendance) is unique as an example of an interior in the Second Rococo style.

The Small Reception Room

Here visitors can see some splendid furniture decorated with porcelain insets and bronze mounts.

On the first floor the decoration of most of the rooms is notably restrained and austere. The furniture is strictly functional and includes tables, chairs, armchairs and desks made in Russia from mahogany in the 1820s and '30s. Only the Bedroom and Study of Maria Fiodorovna, the wife of Alexander III, are more showily stylish. The exquisite harmonious study was decorated by Robert (Roman) Melzer in the Moderne (Russian Art Nouveau) style. On display

The Large Reception Room

The Vestibule

Nicholas I's Maritime Study

here is a splendid collection of glass, porcelain and silver articles that belonged to Maria Fiodorovna, with a special place in it going to pieces from the celebrated Copenhagen Porcelain Factory in her native Denmark.

On the top, attic, floor of the palace there is the Maritime Study of Nicholas I. The chief element in its decoration is the illusionist painting by V. Dodonov that reproduces the drapery of a military tent. The Study has a balcony with a view of the Gulf of Finland. From here Nicholas I would watch naval manoeuvres, giving instructions through a loudhailer to be relayed by the semaphore tower on the shore.

Bronze statue of Glory. *Sculptor: Christian Daniel Rauch.*
First half of the 19th century

The Farm Palace

THE HISTORY of the Farm Palace goes back to the late 1820s when on Nicholas I's instructions the architect Adam Menelaws included in the Alexandria ensemble a small elegant pavilion adjoining the Farm that was intended as a summer residence for the young heir to the throne, the future Alexander II. Otto von Bismarck, who visited Alexandria in 1835, found the Farm "got up with taste not unlike a Swiss house with a path leading from it through a romantic valley... to the dwelling of the heir's parents."

The Large Study of Alexander Nikolayevich, the Heir to the Throne

The Study of Empress Maria Alexandrovna

Mahogany étagère. *Russia. 1840–60*

Later the pavilion was enlarged several times by the architect Andrei Stakenschneider, acquiring an ever-grander appearance. The last work was done on it in 1858–60.

All the alterations produced elegant comfortable apartments for Alexander II, Empress Maria Alexandrovna and their children – drawing-rooms, studies, dressing-rooms and nurseries.

Today the interiors of the ground floor of the palace have been reconstructed. The first room there is Maria Alexandrovna's spacious reception room with a bay window. Next comes Alexander II's reception room with mahogany and walnut furniture made in the "Nicholas I Empire style" by Russian craftsmen.

Then, by way of a small corridor, visitors enter the grand Blue Study of Alexander II, the largest room in the palace. The décor of the Study is a romantic stylization in the spirit of mediaeval European castles. The stuccowork is notable for its variety and expressiveness. The furniture is a set supplied by the court maker Andrei Tur in waxed dark oak – an example of the Neo-Gothic of the mid-1850s.

Casket. *Ebony, ivory. 19th century*

Maria Alexandrovna's Dressing Room

It was in the Blue Study at the Farm Palace that Alexander II's great reforms were planned, the most notable of which was the abolition of serfdom. The room contains a painting of the Tsar-Liberator by Ivan Kramskoi, one of the greatest portraitists of the second half of the nineteenth century.

Empress Maria Alexandrovna's apartments begin with the Drawing-Room that stands out for the light elegance of its decoration. Visitors' attention is caught by the painted leaf ornament on the ceiling and the moulded frieze featuring the arms of Alexandria. A major role in the décor is played by the cotton fabric with a bright floral pattern that was used for the drapes on the windows and doors and to upholster the furniture. On display here is a fine collection of Meissen porcelain, mainly figurines, from the mid-1700s, when that factory was at its peak.

The Empress's apartments also include a Dining-Room furnished in the Biedermeier style and Maria Alexandrovna's Study with a five-sided bay window, which is the most exquisitely decorated room in the female part of the palace. The interior of the Study was created in 1838–41 and painted by the decorative artist Medici. The Empress used the study for receiving members of the imperial family and her guests. Among the small circle of people close to Maria Fiodorovna were the poets Alexei Konstantinovich Tolstoi, Piotr Viazamesky and Fiodor Tiutchev, who all dedicated verses to her.

Mirror in the Dressing Room

The Drawing-Room

The Valet's Room with a spiral staircase to the upper floor

The Empress's apartments end with the Bedroom, the Dressing-Room (decorated by Stakenschneider in 1838–41) and the only service room on the ground floor, which was used by the maid-of-honour in attendance on the Empress.

The Dining-Room

Inside the Chapel

res of the apostles Paul, with
roll, and Peter, with the keys.
*per. Sculptor: Vasily Demuth-
Malinovsky*

The Gothic Chapel

THE GOTHIC CHAPEL (Church of St Alexander Nevsky) was the domestic church of Emperor Nicholas I's family. It stands next to the Farm Palace on a site immediately adjoining the eastern boundary of the Lower Park. With its integral volume, harmonious proportions and fine silhouette the Chapel reminds one of the mediaeval cathedrals of Germany and France.

The history of the building goes back to 1829, when Nicholas I on a visit to Berlin commissioned a design for a church from the eminent Prussian architect Karl Friedrich Schinkel. The foundation stone was laid on 24 May 1831 and on 3 July 1834, "in the presence of Their Imperial Majesties, the entire imperial family, the Crown Prince of Prussia and his wife", the finished building was consecrated. The Chapel is adorned by 43 figures of angels, the Virgin and Child, evangelists and saints chased from copper sheeting following models by the sculptor Vasily Demuth-Malinovsky. The carved and gilded iconostasis with Gothic ornament inside the Chapel contains icons by the eminent academic painter Timofei Neff.

The Ruin Bridge on the
way from the Cottage to
the Farm Palace and
Gothic Chapel

A ceramic vase in the Upper Garden

Peter I's Palace at Strelna

STRELNA — is an ensemble located a few kilometres east of Peterhof and 22½ kilometres from St Petersburg. It comprises the wayside estate of Peter the Great with a small wooden palace (1718) and the Konstantinovsky Palace that was reconstructed in 2003 and transferred to the Administration of the President of the Russian Federation.

The first mention of Strelna in Peter I's Campaign Journal is dated 2 November 1706. Then, on 13 January 1711, the Tsar instructed Alexander Menshikov to build at Strelna "a couple of log cabins, a livestock and poultry farm and a small pond for keeping fish". The identity of the original designer of Peter's wooden house remains unknown.

In 1719–20 it was reconstructed to a plan by Jean-Baptiste Le Blond, becoming the centre of a small park, which had exemplary gardens and hothouses. In 1750, on the orders of Empress Elizabeth, Peter I's daughter, the dilapidated palace of her father was dismantled and thoroughly restored by the architect Francesco Bartolomeo Rastrelli. Today the reconstructed interiors of the building make it possible to sense the atmosphere of Peter the Great's time. This is a great triumph for the researchers of the Peterhof Museum Preserve and the restoration specialists.

The Drawing-Room

Costume worn by Peter I.
Broadcloth, silk, gold thread.
Berlin, Germany.
1720s

The Dining-Room

The cosy ground floor of the palace is an ensemble of eight fairly small comfortable rooms that have moulded fireplaces, tiled stoves and furniture made from precious varieties of wood in Russia and Europe in the second half of the seventeenth and eighteenth centuries. Here too are some of Peter the Great's personal belongings and works from his own collections of paintings and applied art.

The largest room in the palace is the Grand Hall that was created to Le Blond's design in a specially added second storey. It has a floor area of 85 square metres, over 900 square feet. On the south it is adjoined by the upper landing and on the north there is a balcony with a view of a grove that has a cutting through it in the direction of the sea. The successfully struck proportions, the light-coloured walls and the large windows that go down almost to the floor give the hall a sense of restrained ostentation. The walls are hung with paintings — large Biblical scenes, battle pieces, landscapes and others.

The Bedroom

Little divan in the Passage Room. *First half of the 19th century*

ORANIENBAUM

ORANIENBAUM is one of the many estates that belonged to Peter the Great's closest comrade in arms – Prince Alexander Menshikov. It is located on the shore of the Gulf of Finland opposite Kotlin Island where Menshikov was supervising the construction of the Kronslot fort. The name of the estate probably comes from the German for "orange tree" (Orangenbaum). Today it is a unique monument of the eighteenth century, almost untouched by later reconstruction.

Menshikov began to construct Oranienbaum in the early 1710s. The first plan for the estate is believed to have been drawn up by the Italian architect Giovanni Maria Fontana who left Russia in 1713, after which the project was entrusted to Johann Gottfried Schädel, whom Menshikov had hired in Germany. Thanks to Schädel's efforts in the 1710s and '20s a magnificent ensemble was created at Oranienbaum with the impressive Great Palace and a terraced garden. A navigable canal led from the Gulf of Finland to the palace, ending in a small harbour. To the east of the palace the River Karost (or Karasta) was dammed, creating the picturesque Lower Pond that was known at the time as "the Little Amusement Sea" on which Menshikov kept a "flotilla" of pleasure boats.

The Great Menshikov Palace

The Picture Cabinet in Peter III's Palace in Peterstadt

AFTER Menshikov was banished to Siberia in 1727, Oranienbaum belonged for a time to the naval department, before in the early 1740s it was given to Empress Elizabeth's nephew Peter Fiodorovich (originally Karl Peter Ulrich of Holstein-Gottorp, the future Peter III), whom the Empress had designated as her heir and to whom she granted Oranienbaum as a country residence. Peter and his wife, Catherine Alexeyevna (originally Princess Sophie Friederike Auguste of Anhalt-Zerbst, the future Catherine II), spent every summer from 1746 to 1761 at Oranienbaum, making it the summer capital of their "little court".

Chinoiserie painting on the doors of the Picture Hall

Peter III

Francesco Bartolomeo Rastrelli was dispatched to set the estate in order and he carried out a reconstruction of the Great Palace. Soon he was replaced by Antonio Rinaldi who completed the facelift of the palace and built for Grand Duke Peter the "amusement fortress" of Peterstadt with a miniature palace inside it.

In the 1760s and '70s, after Peter III had been deposed, Rinaldi continued work at Oranienbaum. He created the unique ensemble of Catherine II's Private Dacha, the land for which she had bought while still a grand duchess. The heart of this ensemble was a regular park that extended for a distance of 600 metres. On its northern edge stood Rastrelli's Stone Hall, while on the south Rinaldi constructed the incomparable Chinese Palace with a small landscape park.

The dacha ensemble also included the Coasting Hill (1762–74). This magnificent piece of architecture and engineering was an early version of the rollercoaster. It once extended some 530 metres but today only the

Peter III's Palace in Peterstadt

The Porcelain Cabinet in the Coasting Hill Pavilion

enchantingly beautiful pavilion survives. The 33-metre-high three-storey building has three projections decorated with colonnades. It is famous for its interiors: the Vestibule with a winding staircase with an openwork balustrade, the central Round Hall and the Porcelain Cabinet, for the decoration of which Catherine II had forty porcelain groups made at the Meissen factory from models by Johann Joachim Kändler. Some of the ceramic compositions were devoted to Russia's victories in the Russo-Turkish war. The walls, vaults and floors inside the pavilion are lined with artificial marble and painted with a fine elegant design that makes them resemble porcelain. This is the only place in Russia where you can see artificial marble floors (150 square metres in area).

The Chinese Palace is the heart of the Private Dacha and one of Rinaldi's most original creations. It gets its name from two small rooms, cabinets decorated in the chinoiserie (imitation Chinese) style that was popular in the Rococo era. The parquet floors in the Chinese Palace produced to Rinaldi's designs have a total area over more than 700 square metres and are striking for their richness and variety of patterns. They were assembled from fifteen kinds of wood, including pear, maple, rosewood, sandalwood, lemon, tobacco tree, palms, boxwood, palisander and yew. The suspended ceilings with broad coving running smoothly into relatively small paintings and the interior walls are decorated with gilded mouldings as well as ornamental

The Coasting Hill Pavilion

The Hall of the Muses in the Chinese Palace

and figurative murals with a wide range of motifs executed by Stefano Torelli, Diziani, Barozzi, Sampsoy, Rotari and others on mythological, allegorical and pastoral themes. Particularly splendid are the painted panels by Barozzi and Torelli that adorn the walls of Catherine II's Golden Study.

In 1796 Oranienbaum became the property of the new heir to the throne, Grand Duke Alexander Pavlovich (the future Alexander I). His wife, Yelizaveta Alexeyevna, was fond of spending the summer here. In 1826 the estate passed

The Chinese Palace

The Large Chinese Cabinet in the Chinese Palace

to Alexander's brother, Grand Duke Mikhail Pavlovich and right up to the revolution it was owned by his descendants, the Dukes of Mecklenburg- Strelitz.

During the Second World War Oranienbaum managed to escape being occupied and as a result its palaces are the only ones in the suburbs of St Petersburg that can boast authentic eighteenth-century interiors.

PROJECT COORDINATOR:
V. Korshunova

AUTHORS:
V. Korshunova
N. Ryzhova
S. Khilkevich
I. Tsapovetskaya
O. Shchebuniayeva

TRANSLATOR:
P. Williams

EDITOR:
T. Lobanova

DESIGNER:
A. Lobanov

PHOTOGRAPHERS:
B. Baranovsky
V. Davydov
P. Demidov
V. Denisov
A. Kasnitsky
A. Lobanov
V. Savik
G. Semenov
Ye. Siniaver
O. Trubsky
P. Ushanov
G. Shablovsky

3D PLAN ARTIST:
A. Smirnov

*Materials from the
collection of the
Peterhof State Museum
Preserve have been
used in the publication*

ПЕТЕРГОФ
© PETERHOF STATE
MUSEUM PRESERVE
www.peterhofmuseum.ru

AMFORA
MEDIA LTD.

© OOO AMFORA
ST PETERSBURG

2011
www.amforamedia.ru
www.amforamedia.com

Plan
of the Great
Cascade

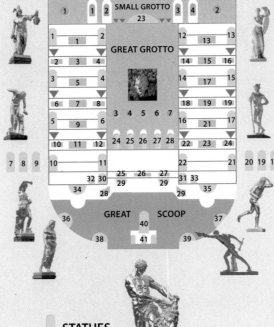

BUSTS
1. Spring
2. Summer
3. Autumn
4. Winter

MASKS
1. Bacchus
2. Neptune
3–7. Masks on the arches of the Great Grotto

STATUES
1. Perseus
2. Pandora
3. Ceres
4. Capitoline Faun
5. Florentine Faun
6. Callipygean Venus
7. Belvedere Meleager
8. Bacchus and a Satyr
9. Medici Venus
10. Jupiter
11. Capitoline Flora
12. Acis
13. Juno
14. Faun
15. Galatea
16. Venus de'Medici
17. Capitoline Mercury
18. Capitoline Antinous
19. Germanicus
20. Discus thrower
21. Actaeon
22. Ganymede
23. Tritons
24. Pan and Olympus
25. Callipygean Venus
26. Barberini Faun
27. Bacchus
28. Cupid and Psyche
29. Shell Fountains
30, 31. Borghese Wrestlers
32, 33. Frogs
34. Allegory of the Neva
35. Allegory of the Volkhov
36, 37. Sirens
38, 39. Naiads with Tritons
40. Samson
41. Lion heads

BAS-RELIEFS
1. Pluto abducting Proserpine
2, 4, 8, 16, 22, 24. Narcissus
3. Hippomenes throwing apples to Atlanta
5, 13, 21. The Centaur Nessus attempting to rape Deianeira
6. A Triton abducting an infant
7, 15, 23. Neptune on the seashore
9. The Triumph of Amphitrite
10. Pan with a Satyr and Cupids
11. Neptune in a sea chariot
12, 20. Perseus rescuing Andromeda
14. A Triton abducting a woman
17. Diana and Actaeon
18. Phaeton falling from the heavens
19. Contest between Apollo and Marsyas in playing the musical instruments
25. Sacrifice
26. Latona and Lycian peasants
27. Venus on the seashore
28, 29. The Rape of Europa

VASES